Entering the Tao

Entering the Tao

Master Ni's Guidance for Self-Cultivation

Hua-Ching Ni

SHAMBHALA
BOSTON & LONDON
1997

Shambhala Publications, Inc.
Horticultural Hall
300 Massachusetts Avenue
Boston, Massachusetts 02115
www.shambhala.com

9 8 7 6 5

Printed in the United States of America
⊗ This edition is printed on acid-free paper that meets
the American National Standards Institute z39.48 Standard.
Distributed in the United States by Random House, Inc.,
and in Canada by Random House of Canada Ltd

Library of Congress Cataloging-in-Publication Data
Ni, Hua-Ching.
    Entering the Tao: Master Ni's guidance for self-cultivation/
Hua-ching Ni.
        p. cm.
    Includes bibliographical references.
    ISBN 1-57062-161-6 (alk. paper)
    1. Spiritual life—Taoism. 2. Tao. I. Title.
BL1923.N53518 1997   96-36971
299'.51444—dc21   CIP

Before, you were at the fence.
You will soon be at the gate.
Maybe you will want to enter the hall.
Perhaps you would like to go to the outer room
and then sit in the inner room and enjoy the use
of the invaluable treasures.

Contents

Contents

Contents

Editor's Preface

Hua-Ching Ni is a Taoist master who has been teaching in the United States since 1976. He has devoted his life to continuing a spiritual tradition transmitted through an unbroken succession of seventy-four generations of masters dating back to the Han dynasty (206 BCE–220 CE). Trained in mainland China by Taoist masters in healing, T'ai Chi Ch'uan, Kung Fu, Internal Alchemy, Chinese medicine, and herbology, he is a fully acknowledged master of all aspects of Taoist arts and metaphysics. However, he says that he prefers to be thought of simply as a spiritual friend.

Master Ni is the author of more than forty-five books in English on philosophy, Chinese medicine, T'ai Chi Ch'uan, the *I Ching*, Taoist meditation, and related subjects. In his writings he uses straightforward language and personal experiences, as well as traditional stories and teachings of the ancient masters, to impart the wisdom of Taoism—or, as he calls it, the Integral Way. His teachings promote a simple, natural, healthy, and happy way of life that lays the foundation for spiritual self-cultivation. Master Ni emphasizes that it is important to first establish a good understanding of basic spiritual principles and then begin to realize this wisdom in daily life by adopting practices and attitudes that help to conserve, nourish, and refine the subtle energy. The selections in this book, drawn from the large body of Master Ni's writings, were chosen so as to emphasize these two areas of principles and practice, with an emphasis on teachings that are both inspiring and easy to understand.

Several meditations and other practices are included among the selections. Readers should be aware that Taoist practices, although apparently very simple, can also be quite powerful, and it is usually recommended that one practice only under the guidance of a qualified teacher. If you try the practices described in this book, please do so sensibly and with moderation, and understand that the publisher and author cannot be held responsible for any ill effects resulting from improper use of the exercises.

I am a great admirer of Master Ni and feel that spiritual seekers of all kinds can benefit from his words. Since the book is meant to be an introductory sampler rather than a complete presentation of Master Ni's work, readers are encouraged to consult the books listed in "Sources and Resources," where information is also given on where to obtain further information about studying the Integral Way. At the end of each selection in the book, the source in the bibliography is identified by number, followed by the page citation.

Kendra Crossen Burroughs

Entering the Tao

Treasure the Tao

I would like to share some very useful advice for your personal cultivation. Taoist self-cultivation is a mental discipline in which every single thought must respond only to Tao, the oneness of the universe. Do ordinary people's thoughts respond to Tao? No, because ordinary people only think about the trivialities of daily life, and then wonder why they are troubled and unhappy. Will they ever find happiness this way? No, for there is no end to troubles in the human sphere. Even in meditation, if you review all your activities and troubles you will just keep making them recur. What is the method to achieve lasting peace and harmony in life? You must work persistently to reach the spiritual level, even if you have no experience of its existence.

Tao is the potency of the universe. It includes all Gods, all deities, all divine beings, all spirits, and all souls. This means that all things have Tao as their deep root. Anyone who embraces Tao also embraces the potency of the Universe. To embrace Tao is to become Tao, and nothing can be beyond you, nothing can occupy you.

In the sphere of life, individuals may die and transform into other things, but Tao does not change, because it *is* the change. That which does not change into something else can only be the absolute Tao. Tao is the root of everything, but everything is not Tao. To be formed, limited, manifested, and definable is to be something; to be not limited, defined or formed is Tao.

To use your good mind to respond to trouble is a waste. It is true that the achieved ones know that nothing is beyond

Tao, including the trivialities of daily life. However, they never regret anything and they also never really become attached to anything either.

So do not lose yourself in the details of life. There will always be some things in your life you do or do not like, but they are only a small aspect of your life. Life is whole; it is only by attaching yourself to the pieces that you become narrow, shallow, and partial. Do not let your life be cut into pieces by worldly attractions. Do not live for such things and you will stop segmenting yourselves.

A person of Tao is a person of wholeness. He or she embraces the wholeness of Tao, not an image of God, not one single doctrine of any spiritual path, not life, not death, not anything that occupies the mind. By harmonizing with the Tao you will be aligned with the universal potency.

Be a man or woman of potency, not a person who undermines their life by destructive thinking, attitudes, and behavior. Be a person who does not become a "self-robber." Tao cannot be taught to ordinary people because they keep thieves in their minds. They fasten to their ignorance and the limitations of their own self-indulgence. A person of Tao treasures only Tao and focuses only on Tao.

We presume to title ourselves as a man or woman of Tao, or a friend of Tao. However, we are all the children of Tao. If we say we are the offspring of a certain person or family, we cut ourselves off from the great root which is Tao. Although we came through others, they were only beings, not the source of life. In other words, unless people clearly recognize the source of their lives, they will blindly devitalize themselves by becoming "self-robbers."

One can ask, "Is God the source?" If so, then God must have some shape. If he is formed, then he is no different than we are; he is only one of the offspring. Tao is the final source, the unformed origin of all things. Things created can only be changed or re-formed. There is no one creator of the universe, there was no particular design or laws which existed before-hand, there was only the primal energy. Things manifest through spontaneity. Spontaneity is the way of living things. Rigidity is the way of death.

Man's real disaster came about when he lost his naturalness. How? He started to build an artificial conceptual world. People may ask, "If man is to be natural, why should he even bother to wear clothes?" Actually, clothes are a natural extension of our skin. It is not the clothes that are unnatural or bad, but excessive materialism which is unnatural. Anything is right if it is a correct expression of spontaneity. Unfortunately, people today have lost their natural spontaneity as a result of living amid the contention and rivalry of modern society.

The Tao is really simple; it is people who make it complicated. They must awaken from the complications they have created for themselves and dare to live a plain and truthful natural life. [8:137–39]

Zero Doctrine

What does zero doctrine mean? The general understanding of the word *zero* is "nothing," so from the words *zero doctrine* you might almost believe that there is no doctrine. That is actually almost close to the teaching of Tao, because Tao does not emphasize any point of view. It is neutral, like zero. It does not hold any particular standpoint which would create a prejudicial tendency. It rejects any possible extremes. Therefore, the zero doctrine is one way to understand or define what is Tao.

However, if we continue talking this way, then you will

mistakenly believe that there is nothing to Tao and you will mistakenly believe that you are wasting your time by studying it and wishing to learn it. Actually, there is everything to Tao and it is the most important learning, no matter how you come to understand it. To help you understand, I need to further develop this point.

At the beginning, Tao just meant "the Way." Tao is the ancient spiritual education. It was especially emphasized about twenty-five hundred years ago, when the wise people of society reacted to the confusion of the time. In order to help people, they took their wisdom and spiritual knowledge, which was an internal understanding, and put it into words or concepts so that they would be able to explain it to people. There were several different teachers, and as they taught, students came and schools were formed. At that time, the most popular school was Mo Tzu's school. It was the continuation of ancient Taoism. The way he worded his internal, intuitive understanding was to suggest to people that all people return to the faith of impartial Heaven by following the Heavenly Way. You must understand that he was talking about a good spiritual life, not a place with clouds or some impersonal and uncaring giant. He was talking about heeding one's own spiritual wisdom or internal energy awareness or conscience. He meant that one should be fair in every circumstance and not favor one person over another. No individual human life should be emphasized above another.

Another school that was popular at that time was the Yang school. Some people categorize Yang Tzu's teachings as belonging to the Taoist school, but they are mistaken, because his teaching was quite different. Yang Tzu's philosophy is similar in attitude to hedonism, a teaching of ancient Greece. Yang Tzu emphasized that life is short and the mission of life is to enjoy oneself to the greatest extent. He believed that a person's enjoyment is more important than anything else. By this theory, naturally the followers of Yang Tzu conduct their lives so that they enjoy much sensory excitement. They do not talk about what is truth and not truth, or about any responsibility or duty, tomorrow or yesterday. They talk about what they can enjoy physically now.

At the time, those teachings were popular. Even Confucius's last student, Menfucius, wrote that the majority of people seeking awakening considered themselves to be either Moist or Yangist. But Menfucius never mentioned the Taoist school in his writings, because he himself absorbed some teaching and practice from the ancient teaching of Tao. So you can see that the other achieved Taoists at that time still managed themselves with coolness and calmness: they stayed at the side and did not become involved with the changing waves of popular Chinese society.

However, Confucianism also developed its teachings. Confucianism came after the time of Mo and Yang. It wished to use regulations, customs, family systems, and a system of monarchy to bring order to the society as was done in previous times. The students of Confucius were ambitious to reform society through rules.

Inevitably, these three schools argued a lot because their points of view were so very different. All of this disturbance and stimulation finally aroused the aged Lao Tzu, an achieved Taoist. He responded to the challenge of the situation and wrote his book, the *Tao Teh Ching*. He gave it as a gift to an officer at a border checkpoint when he left the central society. The man appreciated Lao Tzu's teaching, so Lao Tzu gave the book to him and left the noisy society to look for peace and quiet. Mo Tzu, Confucius, Lao Tzu, and Chuang Tzu all presented the Integral Spirit with a different emphasis. All of them took the duty of awakening and harmonizing the people, but the approach was different. Thereby, the pure Taoism, different from the religious type of Taoism, took the duty of awakening people of spiritual differences to the subtle truth, Tao.

You are probably wondering how the teachings of these three schools give respect to zero doctrine. Well, if you read the *Tao Teh Ching* carefully—which I highly recommend— you will notice that at the beginning Lao Tzu mentions that the truth is nothing. He does not mean there is no truth. He means that truth is not-a-thing. Not only does he mention that at the beginning, but he repeats it all the way through the book. So the ultimate truth is not something that can be defined by a set of words. What is definable is an individual's personal view, temperament, quality of mind, education, feelings, and sensations. All of those things come together to present an individual's understanding, concepts, and definition of truth if he starts to talk about it. But that is still not the truth. In other words, if you are going to define the truth, your definition does not define the truth; it defines your viewpoint of the truth. The ultimate truth, as Tao, can never be defined.

I write my books to give viewpoints of many of the ancient developed ones. Why? I do it because I hope that after reading and understanding many different viewpoints of Tao from the achieved ones, you will come to understand what the words cannot define. Your understanding of Tao will not actually be a set of words. It will be deeper than words.

The beginning of the *Tao Teh Ching* points out the oneness and the unity of truth. The second chapter shows that everything has two sides, and the two sides help each other. The third chapter continues to say that even if all things have two sides, it is still important to have a mature attitude. People still need to reach maturity from their intellectual or conceptual development, which can be endless.

So all the arguments between the three schools, or between any points of view, or set of words, are not necessary. They are only different viewpoints of the same undiscussible thing. In a sense, they are all true, but none of them are exactly true, because Tao can never really be defined. It is like trying to define lunch to a hungry person. You can talk about the ingredients and the colors, the temperatures of the food, and so on, but his listening to a description of it is not the same as actually sitting down and eating it himself. So why do I spend a lot of time writing books to talk about it? To help stimulate your appetite for it. You see, it is so much better than an ordinary meal; if you do not whet your appetite for it, you might settle for something much less.

So a wise one does not argue about how he defines Tao, because he knows that each person views things from the standpoint of age, sex, personal growth, experience, education, and so forth. These differences between people cannot be solved by argument. Arguments about Tao usually occur only about words, not about the underlying reality behind them. . . .

So far, I have not yet explained what the zero doctrine means. I will give an example of it so that you can understand. In almost every classroom, there is a blackboard. When a teacher teaches something, in order to help the student understand better, he sometimes needs to draw a diagram on the blackboard. Once the blackboard is all written over, what does he do? He wipes it clean to make it ready again for the next use. That is called zero doctrine. It means to return to stillness, purity, nothing, or zero. Zero means a point between negative and positive. For example, when we drive a car, we can put it in neutral. When we put it in neutral, it is at the point of being able to go either in drive (forward) or in reverse. It is the empty balance point at which a clear decision can be made. When we teach zero doctrine, we mean to teach you to return to the point of clarity and keep your mind flexible. But if you have already put a doctrine there, it means your flexibility of mind is already given up. You are fixed to that doctrine rather than looking for progress or growth. That is where a person dies, if he sticks to it. If you have a flexible mind, you can correct your mind about a situation, renew your mind, develop your mind, and find a new replacement idea or solution.

Tao cannot be defined by the differences between what is in front and what is in back. Nor is this the Taoist mind. A healthy Taoist attitude always comes back to a neutral point. For example, once we notice that we have thoughts or emotions toward a certain thing or person, once we have built any kind of attitude toward something, we always need to put it aside to come back to the zero point. We must always be waiting for change. A stiffened attitude will prevent change or improvement from happening; an attitude of neutral or zero will provide the flexibility to flow with a situation, however it occurs. We cannot hold an already formalized, established, or stiffened impression, memory, or record of an attitude that we have already established toward something. Those things prevent positive movement, growth, or change. . . .

There is contention and conflict among people on a big scale and small scale. The most meaningless trouble is caused by holding ready-made ideas. It happens if someone does not return to the zero point, or if someone does not know the value of the zero point. The truth of Tao is the zero point, the point where anything can be produced. It gives birth to all things. Do you catch this point, spiritually?

It is important for people to have kindness. People can learn from those who have kindness to restore their flexibility of mind. Do not learn from people who produce and hold toxins. Eventually the toxins attack your heart. In the world, we see that there are so many toxic-minded people. But few people can restore their fresh, alive, elastic mind. As students of the zero doctrine, we truly know the value of the elastic mind. You see, all life comes from no life. All ideas come from no idea. All religion comes from no religion. Everything started at the zero point. . . .

Because things in the world change, there is no reason to hold tightly on to any teaching or establishment that began two or three thousand years ago. Only the helpful principles that were taught should be followed, because principles do not change. All good principles can merge together as one good unified principle that exists prior to any of the momentary teachings that were developed. It is Tao. A good example is any principle which is able to return to zero once it has done its job.

Yet, in the zero doctrine, there is no excitement. It is not thrilling, but it is really truthful. It is really healthy, like eating tofu or soy products.

However unexciting, this is my message. [21:119–26]

What My Mother Taught Me

Tao is realized in everyday life. When I was a teenager, I gathered a group of young children in my neighborhood as my followers. They liked to sit there listening to what I said because I had learned the tongue of my father and teachers. I was proud of that. In doing so, however, I often neglected my duty as a family member. I lived upstairs by myself, and the rest of the family lived downstairs. At mealtime, I made the whole family wait for me to come down because I was in meditation, studying the holy books and scripts, and I continued doing that.

One day, I really upset my mother because it was a cold day and the food she had prepared was best eaten warm. I always made my family eat cold food because of my tardiness. My mother thought it was not proper for me to do that, so she decided to give me a lesson. She said to me, "You think quoting lofty phrases from the books is Tao. You keep meditating upstairs in your own room and call it Tao. You think reading those books will make you the friend of the sages. You think it is Tao, but it is not Tao. It is your personal enjoyment. You know, when I was young, I was similar, having fanatic thoughts about Tao, and I also behaved like you. I thought that what was everyday and mundane was really secular and unholy. But then I really was enlightened to know what Tao is, so I married your father and gave birth to you four children. Since then, I understand that to give birth to children is Tao. To raise them is Tao. To feed them is Tao. To change their diapers is Tao. To make clothes is Tao. Everything in life that you do seriously and find meaning in is Tao. Anything beyond the necessary duty, contribution, and positive attitude toward life is not Tao.

"If I did not think it was Tao, why give birth to you? Why do I keep the daily routine of washing, cutting, cooking, and serving the vegetables and the other food, waiting for all of you to come to eat? I do it because I think that is earnest life. At no time do I cheat myself. So I make a connection with heaven. I am self-respecting. I credit what I am doing. I think my life is righteous, I do not take advantage of anybody. I am not dependent upon anybody: I do my part, do my share, and by living so, I do not need to consider whether I have Tao or need to attain Tao or anything else. You think that just reading and gathering people to listen to you is Tao. That is not practicing Tao."

This is what my mother taught me. So if a person truly understands Tao, he does not insist on the formality. He can teach Tao and apply Tao in any occasion in his daily work and life.

The fish lives in water, but one day the fish says, "I need to attain Tao. I need to move to the mountain." This is a bad choice. He cannot live on the mountain. He leaves the Tao to look for some self-expansion. The great path, the great principle of spiritual cultivation, is to maintain your balance, maintain your good concentration in everyday life, like holding a bowl of water and walking in the dark. If you do not balance yourself well, if you do not have a strong sense of morality, if you hit anything, you will spill the water. This is the value of spiritual cultivation: enlightening yourself to see through your own darkness, to maintain your balance. This is the first principle a person needs to achieve. Then we can talk about the other high achievements and development. [21:9–10]

What Is Tao?

Many people ask me, what is Tao? Is it not clear enough? Tao is integral truth. It is not a projection of a prejudice; it is not a partial truth that needs insistence; it is not a viewpoint or a philosophy. It is the universal integral truth, the truth of all lives, the truth that exists prior to any thought or statement. You may not be familiar with the terminology, but it does not matter. A name for the truth, a language for the reality, a picture of a person, a title of the spirit, helps some, but it is not real. It is just as you make it, but the program is really your limitation. Names, titles, special vocabularies, pictures, or images may help some people's lives, but they are still not spiritual reality. They are what people make of them. All such established religious programs are ultimately limitations. Once you break away from these poor psychological skills you are attached to, the openness and broadness lets you become spiritually all-reachable, all-approachable. If you are all-reachable or all-approachable spiritually, you embrace the entire spiritual world and the entire spiritual world embraces you. There is no separation.

Integral truth is not a uniting of all religions; it is doing away with all religions. Use your mind to directly reach the universal mind. Use your spirit to directly reach the universal spirit. Surely in human life, religion is a matter of different customs in different societies. Achieved ones never disagree with customs and also never agree with any custom. They live, they are happy, and they may enjoy the customs, but their spiritual development is never limited or confined by them. An integral person is a directly achieved person of integral truth. This person embraces integral truth without conflicting with or becoming prejudiced by the customs of the society in which he or she was raised.

Subscribing to most religions is like getting on a bus that promises to take the undeveloped souls to a different camp. But it turns out to be a concentration camp. You need to choose a spot to get off, otherwise the end of the ride is where you end your life. It is better to choose spiritual education which makes you wise and able to manage your life.

Learn the universal spiritual education of Tao, which helps you attain spiritual independence. Spiritually, you are self-responsible. Spiritually, you do not need another ruler or authority to set you in good order or to straighten out your life. This you can do yourself by learning from the universal spiritual education of Tao. [16:142–43]

Yin and Yang

Yin/yang is the Way of Heaven and Earth, the fundamental principle of the myriad things, the father and mother of change and transformation, the root of inception and destruction.

—Su-wen*

The original energy of the universe is fathomless and incomprehensible. It is beyond time and beyond space. Contained within it is all existence and nonexistence. Yet it is neither existence nor nonexistence. The ancient sages in one region of the world named it Tao. Tao, as the Subtle Origin of the universe, brings forth all things, nurtures and sustains them, and then draws them back to return to their subtle source. The ancient achieved ones revealed the subtle truth that the universe has two apparent aspects. One is the unmanifest aspect—the undivided oneness or ultimate nothingness, said to exist "before Heaven and Earth were born." In this aspect, the primal energy of the universe is undifferentiated, absolutely whole and complete. The other aspect is the manifest, perceptible world of multiplicity which is "after Heaven and Earth were born." Although these aspects appear as two, the manifest and the unmanifest are in fact one.

Tao manifests itself through an active process of self-expression. Creation may be viewed as the process in which

---

*The *Su-wen* is the upper volume of the *Yellow Emperor's Internal Book* and discusses the natural foundation of human life. See *The Yellow Emperor's Classic of Medicine: A New Translation of the Neijing Suwen with Commentary,* by Maoshing Ni (Boston: Shambhala Publications, 1995).

the organization of the undifferentiated primal energy occurs. This organization brings about a polarization of the primal energy into two distinct categories called yin and yang. Although the active aspect (yang) occurs first, its presence implies the possibility of a relatively static perspective (yin) from which the action may be perceived. It is impossible to directly experience or absolutely define the quality of an action (yang) in space. It can be perceived only in relation to a solidified perspective (yin) which coincides and corresponds with it.

As an example of this, let us take the shining of the sun, which may be considered the supreme manifestation of the yang aspect of the solar system. It is not possible to determine that the sun is emitting rays as long as these rays do not strike another object. If they strike an object, the rays may be perceived because of changes which may be observed in the object. Any positive statement about the sun's rays depends upon the observations made with reference to the object. Thus the effect stimulated by an action (yang) is confirmed by the solidified, relatively static object (yin) which corresponds with the effect. Through this polarization of activity and form, the primal energy gives birth to the active pole of the cosmos (Heaven) and the substantialized pole (Earth). Where there is one pole, there must also be the other.

The act of creation may be thought of as an expansion of the primal energy outward from a center. However, for organization to take place, there must also be a coinciding, counterbalancing, contractive force. If the forces of centrifugality (yin) and centripetality (yang) were not equally balanced, nothing could exist. The energy would either disperse itself into nothingness or disappear into the center. The critical balance of these two forces is illustrated by the model of the atom. If the tendency of the electrons to propel themselves away from the nucleus of the atom were not counterbalanced by the force of the protons to attract the electrons to the center, the atom would disintegrate. On a much larger scale, this principle functions to hold together the solar system and the galaxies of the universe.

The nature of yin and yang was first recognized by Fu Shi, who is said by some to have lived between six thousand and eight thousand years ago and by others to have lived between 3852 and 2738 B.C.E. The Yellow Emperor (2698–2598 B.C.E.) stated that "the universe is an expression of the interplay and alternation of the two activities of yin and yang." He formulated twelve principles which further elaborate upon this relationship and provide us with an explanation of the absolute laws of nature which govern the universe. These principles are:

1. That which produces and composes the universe is Tao, the undivided oneness or ultimate nothingness.

2. Tao polarizes itself: yang becomes the active pole of the cosmos, yin becomes the solidified pole.

3. Yang and yin are opposites, and each accomplishes the other.

4. All beings and things in the universe are complex aggregates of universal energy composed of infinitely varying proportions of yin and yang.

5. All beings and things are in a dynamic state of change and transformation; nothing in the universe is absolutely static or completed; all is in unceasing motion because polarization, the source of being, is without beginning and without end.

6. Yin and yang attract one another.

7. Nothing is entirely yin or entirely yang; all phenomena are composed of both yin and yang.

8. Nothing is neutral. All phenomena are composed of unequal proportions of yin and yang.

9. The force of attraction between yin and yang is greater when the difference between them is greater, and smaller when it is smaller.

10. Like activities repel one another. The closer the similarity between two entities of the same polarity, the greater the repulsion.

11. At the extremes of development, yin produces yang and yang produces yin.

12. All beings are yang in the center and yin on the surface.

There is no facet of life to which the activities of yin and yang do not apply. Yin and yang express the polar aspects and interrelationship of everything that exists in the universe. Yin and yang have no fixed, explicit definition, which makes the terms virtually untranslatable. Rather, they represent two broad categories of complements, which include the correspondences of negative and positive, destructive and creative, inert and active, gross and subtle, actual and potential. Initially, the terms were used to connote the influences of the moon and sun. Their meaning was naturally extended to include the shady and sunny slopes of a mountain, the northern and southern banks of a river, the dark and sunny seasons, the front and back sides of the body, and the complementary aspects of social groups, including the opposite genders.

Thus, the definition of yin and yang cannot be limited solely to specific entities or cosmological principles or forces. The general overall definitions of the terms are as follows: Yang represents the quality of activity and yin the quality of solidification. The qualities of yin and yang are relative and not absolute. What might be considered yang in relation to one thing may be considered yin in relation to another, and vice versa. Furthermore, there is always yin within yang and yang within yin.

Over the course of time, the terms *yin* and *yang* have acquired a wide variety of associations. Yang generally signifies completion or the accomplishment or conclusion of some operation actively initiated. It implies something inducing action or motion—a stimulus; whereas yin signifies something confirming and responding—a response.

The *Su-wen* says, "That which moves is yang." Thus yang articulates something dynamic or live; yin signifies something reposing or static, something dying off or fading away. Yin as the counterpart of dynamic action corresponds to a static position at which dynamic phenomena appear as substantiated or stabilized, thus becoming perceptible and able to be defined in space. It is only through response that we perceive stimulus. Yang signifies something causing change. Perceptible change is the criterion that lets us infer that "action" has taken place. The yin quality describes something tending to transform a momentary phenomenon into a persistent one; it lets fleeting qualities endure and maintains unchanged. Yang implies creation and generation, whereas yin nourishes and supports growth. Yang implies something developing and expanding. It implies action that tends to expand in all directions from its supposed point of origin, whereas yin signifies something contracting, closing in. Yang signifies something indeterminate and formless which is nevertheless causal and determining. Yin indicates something with perceptible, specific qualities with the potential to be organized and formed.

All the energy manifestations in the universe may be understood in terms of the combinations and interaction of yin and yang. When subtle, positive yang energies meet and connect with gross, negative yin energies, a new manifestation or phenomenon comes forth. On the cosmic scale, we say the Yang Heavenly energies mix with the Yin Earthly energies to create all life. This is the basic pattern of the activity and interaction of all universal energies.

To attain real understanding of this, a student needs to develop powers of insight or intuition. The ancient sages developed brilliant insight through their direct response to the external environment. They discovered that universal primal energy is the Subtle Origin of all manifest beings and things, and that in the sphere where energy exists before taking form, there is nothing which can be described.

CORRESPONDENCES OF YIN AND YANG

yin	yang
Earth	*Heaven*
moon	*sun*
autumn, winter	*spring, summer*
things female	*things male*
cold, coolness	*heat, warmth*
moisture	*dryness*
inside, interior	*outside, surface*
darkness	*brightness*
things small and weak	*things large and powerful*
the lower part	*the upper part*
water, rain	*fire*
quiescence	*movement*
night	*day*
the right side	*the left side*
the west and north	*the east and south*
the front of the body (chest to belly)	*the back of the body (head to tailbone)*
the hours between noon and midnight	*the hours between midnight and noon*

exhaustion	*repletion*
murkiness	*clarity*
development	*incipience*
conservation	*destruction*
responsiveness	*aggressiveness*
contraction	*expansion*

These correspondences can continue ad infinitum. [38:2–7]

T'ai Chi

One time, with the help of my students, I made a T'ai Chi design in the garden out of special grasses and flowers. It was very beautiful, but at that time I traveled often and no one cared for the T'ai Chi diagram in the garden while I was gone, so the lovely garden became a wild place again. When I looked for it and could not find it, some students said that the T'ai Chi had been destroyed. But they did not know that T'ai Chi can never be destroyed. Any creation, important or otherwise, is a T'ai Chi, the result of the harmonization of two kinds of forces: one is the initial idea and the other is the realization of the idea's energy. T'ai Chi itself is the reality of harmony between two kinds of energy. Once the two energies cooperate, something is created which becomes an extension of their T'ai Chi. [42:113]

The Plainness of Enlightenment

Enlightenment is not a doctrine. It is not Jesus or Buddha or Mohammed. When you become enlightened it can come about through a very small or ordinary thing. You see, the most difficult thing for someone to accept is the plainness of their life. To discover magnificence in every moment of a simple life is truly life's greatest reward.

The search for the truth of life is very much like mountain climbing. Your view is determined by how high you have reached. When people reach the top of the mountain, they have to shout to their fellow climbers, "I have reached the top of the mountain, I have arrived at the summit." But if they would only look over their shoulder, they would see another, higher mountain; then another, and yet another beyond that.

Finally, one realizes that the hardest mountain to climb is the plainness of one's own mind. But who can accept that? Everyone is busy climbing all the external mountains for external or even internal self-recognition. No one is satisfied with a plain life. They are always struggling to improve their situation, and the more they struggle, the more they deviate from their real nature. The more information gathered, the more attention attracted; the more wealth accumulated, the more distorted the beauty of an honest heart. It is like too much makeup on your face, making who you really are more and more remote.

When you were in the cradle you had no knowledge, no wealth, no cosmetics. What was wrong with you then? Now that you have spent all these years accumulating information, wealth, and the other trappings of life, I ask you: Are you happier now? Are you improved? Or are you still crying to have someone change your diapers? [7:127–28]

Self-Reliance

This is a great powerful statement from some spiritually achieved ones: "*My life depends on me, not on Heaven.*"

Excessively religious people may think those people had no God, but I don't see it that way. I think that these were spiritually self-responsible people who did not rely on external authority to make themselves behave correctly. They did not relinquish authority over their lives to other people and external circumstances, trading in Heaven's support to become dependent on others. They did what was right and depended upon their own attainment and achievement to see them through life.

This kind of achievement is called spiritual independence, and it is above the realm of ordinary religious followers. I regard it as highly respected elucidation of the Way. [26:26–27]

God

The true spiritually achieved one respects the natural spiritual world without having to personify it with a white or purple robe or a gold crown. That is junk. It is really childish. It is not true. Religions fight each other over the conceptual level of life. Once you formalize God with a certain shape and color and robe, you fight over what is in your mind as opposed to what is in someone else's mind. At the true spiritual level, conceptual vision is both all right and all wrong, until you reach the subtle essence.

It is important, therefore, to know and see the entire universe as one being. The organs of a spiritually achieved person develop their own spiritual energy and spiritual entities, but they all make up one complete spiritual being. It is the same in the universe. You and I are supported by the same universal spiritual energy; the whole thing is God. There is no separate "God" in the realm of integral truth. [14:197]

Solid Ground

A man weakened his eyesight by drinking too much. Once on his way home from town, he was crossing a bridge spanning a dry steambed and stumbled and fell off the edge. His hands held tightly to the railing; he believed that if he loosened his grip, he would fall into the depths and drown. A passerby who was in a hurry remarked, "You do not need to hold on so tight; there is solid ground beneath the bridge."

The man did not believe him and, after clinging to the rail for a long time, he became exhausted. Finally, he let himself drop onto the bed of the stream and discovered that it was indeed solid ground. Getting up, he chuckled, "Why, had I known there was solid ground beneath, I could have spared myself this whole ordeal!"

People have strong faith in religions, and hold on as tight as the man did to this bridge railing. They do not notice that there is safe, dry ground under their own feet where they need to stand firmly. [25:121]

Way to Go

For worldly problems and complications there is only one way to go. I will tell you a story which is a Taoist treasure that can be applied to all the troubles of modern life.

Cook Ting was cutting an ox after a sacrifice to be used as food for Lord Wen of Hui. At every touch of the hand, every heave of the shoulder, every move of the feet, every bend of the knee, he slipped the knife along effortlessly and all was in perfect rhythm as though he were performing the dance of the mulberry grove to the flow of the melody of Yao's music.

"Ah, this is marvelous," said Lord Wen of Hui. "Imagine skill reaching such heights!"

Cook Ting laid down his knife and replied, "What I care about is the natural path which goes beyond skill. When I first began cutting oxen, all I could see was the ox itself. After three years I no longer saw the whole ox. Now I go at it through intuition. Perception and understanding have come to a stop and intuition moves where it wants. I go along with the natural construction, strike in the big hollow places, guide the knife through large openings, and follow things as they are. So I never touch the smallest ligament or tendon, much less the main joints.

"A good cook changes knives once a year, because he cuts. A mediocre cook changes his once a month, because he hacks. I've had this knife of mine for nineteen years and I've cut thousands of oxen with it, yet the blade is as good as new.

"There are spaces between the joints, and the blade of the knife is just as if it had no thickness really. If you insert what has no thickness into such spaces, then there's plenty of room, more than enough for the blade to play about. And after nineteen years, the blade of my knife is still as good as when it first came from the grindstone.

"However, whenever I come to a complicated spot, I size up the difficulties, tell myself to watch out and be careful, keep my eyes on what I am doing, work very slowly and move the knife with the greatest subtlety until the whole thing comes apart like a clod of earth flopping to the ground. I stand there holding the knife and look all around me, my mind completely full with the satisfaction of accomplishing a perfect job, and then I wipe the knife and put it away.

"Excellent," said Lord Wen of Hui. "I have heard the words of Cook Ting and learned how to solve the problems of life!"

The metaphor of the ox represents the stubbornness of the external world before it is tamed. A Taoist does not hold a passive attitude toward the world. You have seen the picture of Lao Tzu riding the ox. The ox does not ride him! In all circumstances we must be patient and have a clear vision of how to handle any situation. I hope you can do it in the same way Cook Ting deftly carved his ox. [8:128–29]

Society

Society is a fish pond in which people live. Keep it clean and peaceful; avoid disturbing it and causing it to be troubled. At the very least, one should choose independence and remain in peace. Undeveloped people cannot do this; therefore, it is a great spiritual merit to guide others to peace.

Society is a fish pond of human lives. Its impulsive leaders wish to drain the water to catch the other fish or poison them so they can catch all of them, but finally their foolish notions and actions bring about their own self-destruction.

Human society was like a fish pond that belonged to no one; it was natural. Then, strong people came to call it their pond and make other people as their fish. They became the owners of the pond and were titled as this monarch or that monarch. They assumed the power to eat any fish they wanted. For the most part, monarchy has been destroyed, but now in some regions collective forces continue to eat the fish.

Society is a fish pond that belongs to no one but itself. If an individual in this society retains his sense of being in a fish pond, he is limited to the evolution of a fish. One must attain spiritual independence from one's small society as well as from the large human society in order to evolve, develop, and grow. One's spiritual growth may not be the same as the rest of the world, so maintain harmony with society and courageously live your own unique way. Most of the time, one needs to conceal one's light so as not to irritate the surrounding environment. [36:41–42]

The World

Before you attain your achievement and enlightenment, the world is a refinery that you can use to refine or consummate yourself; if you do not succeed, you will be smashed by the big pressure of time and turned into ashes. There is no mercy.

Do not follow the world; it has so many people at different stages of growth and with different problems. Also do not make the world follow you; if you do, there are two problems which can occur. First, the expansion of your ego destroys your moral perfection. Second, your dominance harms the subtle organism of the world.

However, you can help the world in various ways without extending your ego. The *Tao Teh Ching* gives us three guidelines: (1) Help its growth without ruling over it, (2) do your duty without putting it under your title or control or calling it your own, and (3) do what is creative and helpful because your own nature is creative and helpful. Do not pursue or obscure your undertakings on the relative sphere and work only for the worldly reward or payment you receive; virtuous fulfillment is in a different category. Radiate a positive influence in the world through your upright life and in turn, choose virtuous models for your own life. Do not be affected by its slow growth. [36:42]

Three Treasures

In *The Tao Teh Ching*, Lao Tzu says, "I have three treasures; the first is to be kind." Are you kind? Perhaps the problem is not that you are not kind, the problem is that you need to guard yourself from people who might treat you unkindly. However, there is the subtle law that rights all wrongs. You can only live your own life honestly and let people be aware by seeing the mirror of their ugliness. You do not need to attack people or correct them by attacking; that only brings more difficulty.

The second treasure of Lao Tzu is "Do not look for

expansion in material enjoyment or emotional indulgence." This is not a moral idea; it is both practical and beneficial to your life to follow this guidance. The expansion of material enjoyment and the endless expansion of emotional indulgence only hasten the self-destructive processes. Are you wise enough to receive this message?

The third treasure of Lao Tzu is not to try to maintain control over other lives. Sometimes we are too assertive or our sense of self is inflated, and we become opinionated and pass judgment on others. One who does this cannot perceive the subtle law; he only sees the small self. If such a person is not racist, he might become a prejudicial nationalist and support endless confrontation. It is proper to search for balance between the two. Once a person wishes to control another, he extends his energy beyond himself to others; he loses balance. [36:121–22]

Intuition

Concentration is a spiritual condition which is important whether you are driving a car or managing your life. Concentration does not mean to concentrate on an external object; it is concentration upon life itself. It is a power of knowing, an intuitive mystical power which is not obtained by language. It is obtained by keeping your awareness upon the subtle actions that occur inside your thoughts, inside your body, inside the immediate ten inches or so that surround you, and inside your environment. With this mystical intuitive power, you know everything, including the sufficiency of your spiritual nature. This is the way to master your life. When you do so, you can allow all things around you to be what they are. In this way, everything can smoothly reach the Subtle Origin. You join the transformation, but at the same time you maintain the centeredness which is untouched by transformation.

So the true master is in your innermost being; however, whatever you accomplish in your life looks like you have nothing to do with it and receives recognition from the mind before it attains spiritual awareness. Having intuitive power is attained by relaxing one's nervous system and quieting the active intellect. This masterly energy will spontaneously respond to a situation and give the advice you need. An example of this happened in a family. One night the young daughter dreamt that the big tree in their yard was going to fall. She saw the picture of the smashed house. So the young daughter, on the second day, found many ways to convince the whole family to go away. The actual disaster happened that night and the house was totally destroyed. What other name can you give this masterly energy in the most critical time of life? By listening to the advice given intuitively by the subtle spirits, you accomplish life and accomplish the surroundings of life without interference. [24:121]

Inspiration

Once I had an interesting experience. I got a cold, but I could not stop seeing patients because the appointments were already made. I was suffering from the cold and sat in my chair in the early morning. My vision started acting; I saw myself doing some sword dancing. Suddenly, I understood that doing sword dancing was the cure for my cold. So I did the sword dancing to force the virus out by a little sweating, got over the suffering, and went back to work.

Similar inspiration comes to me, for my work, writing, or other activities. A positive, busy-minded person can always receive spiritual help if he is quietly listening for it. The attitude of rushing and haste always slows down the expected good harvest. All teachings given were also received in the same way. [24:73]

What I Learned from the Trees

I would like to tell you about what I have learned from the trees. A few weeks ago I went on a walk in a state park. Walking is one of my favorite exercises. On the trail, I saw many big healthy trees and many small trees among them that were dying. A friend told me, "These small trees die because they have no light. The other trees are tall and create a shadow, and it is the lack of light that makes the little ones die." So we learned that a person who does not see light will die.

But what is important is that you notice that your soul grows in the light. Have you ever seen the subtle light? If the soul cannot see the subtle light, the soul has no nutrition, and sooner or later, the soul will wither and die. Just as it is important for a young tree to see the light, it is important for our soul to see the light. That means that each of us needs to see the subtle light, otherwise our life-tree will not grow well. You may be interested in knowing what the subtle light is. I have a special book devoted to this subject which is called *The Uncharted Voyage towards the Subtle Light*. You may be interested in reading it. If you can see the subtle light, I think that your good life is a more assured thing.

I would like to tell you about the trees where I live. I have made a trail on the land, and each morning I have a chance to walk among the trees. There are a number of trees that have died. I used my foot to kick the bark away on one of them, and saw that there were white termites eating the tree. I pondered why it had such a fate. A Chinese proverb says, "First a thing fails, then decay comes." However, although I was educated in traditional Chinese medicine when I was young, it was also necessary to study the modern knowledge of germs and bacteria and how they work and cause trouble in the human body under different conditions. From that knowledge, we understand that each medical problem involves bacteria or germs active in a diseased area of the human body. After learning that, I had difficulty accepting the ancient proverb as truth anymore. Although it says that the thing fails before it becomes corrupted, now we know that even before decay sets in, there are germs and bacteria already starting to eat it, and that is why it fails. This is the new knowledge I obtained from my schooling.

But is that new study truthful? No. Now there is a new doubt. The trees surrounding the infested ones had a strong life force and were growing tall and strong. They are equally open to the opportunity of being exposed to bugs, bacteria, germs, and woodpeckers. The woodpeckers make holes inside the sick trees to take the bugs out. I have witnessed how the woodpecker makes the holes to take out the worms. Now, my new understanding is what we should learn from a tree: once your life force is strong, bugs and bacteria will not attack you. Only if your life force is weakened and withered are you a victim to termites, woodpeckers and similar things. It is important first to have a strong, healthy life force within you; then your strong life can be free from the harmful attacks of insects and bugs.

Is your life force contained within you, maintained well, and protected well in the right way of growth? Do you allow the spiritual termites and bugs and insects and woodpeckers to attack your life force? When your life force is not well, you allow those things to attack and eat you, to bury your life. Would you recognize a spiritual termite? It may be the very thing you believe is helping you. Some external thing that you wished to bring into your life could be the spiritual termite that drains and undermines your life force. Harm could come from your own mental condition; if so, it is an invisible termite that you grow by yourself. That is a sign of danger. Have you noticed? . . .

I have another personal story to tell you about learning life from trees. When I was young, I lived a good life in my hometown in China before the society changed. It was a bountiful, free society, especially in some parts that were not touched by political turmoil. I lived in a town close to a city and close to a village, but the place I enjoyed most was the bamboo grove. I had a lot of time to enjoy the bamboo grove by myself. In my late teens, I learned a lot from the time I spent watching bamboo. First of all, I learned that bamboo is straight; it does not twist or turn like the trunks of other trees. It grows branches too, and the branches that grow are also straight; they do not twist or turn either. So the first thing I learned from bamboo was straightness or being straight. The second thing I learned is that when the bamboo faces pressure from outside elements, it will yield, and even though it yields, it maintains its straightness. Once the pressure is gone, it moves back to restore its position; undaunted, when it moves back, it is still straight. Whatever happens, it stays straight.

Soon after, it was the time of the war. The people who lived in cities or big towns had to go away from the populated areas, because the Japanese soldiers always traveled the main roads near the big cities, and flee to the mountains. When the trouble came to my hometown, everybody needed to move away. I was the one who refused. Why? Because I had learned something from the bamboo. If pressure comes, I may bend; but when the pressure moves away, I can immediately straighten myself. So because of that enlightenment, I refused to move. My folks laughed at me. My elders said, "You are not bamboo. Bamboo is rooted on the land, it cannot move. Your root is on your head, and you can move." I accepted that my learning and experience was incomplete enlightenment, so I moved away. Since then, I am happy my root is in Heaven. I can move to any place fit for a man of Tao to live. [36:97–100]

Fix It

It may seem to a spiritual person that self-cultivation is an endless enterprise. The original term was "cultivate Tao." Cultivation in Chinese is *sho, sho tao. Sho* means to fix something. Therefore, self-cultivation is self-fixing or adjusting. When do you need to fix something? When you have a problem. Sometimes you wish to accomplish something and achieve a goal. It is correct to have appropriate goals in your life. In working to fulfill your goal, you may feel that your physical strength, intelligence, experience, knowledge, or social support is insufficient or lacking. When such a feeling of insufficiency emerges, there is some fixing that needs to be done. Most people only look at what they wish to get; they do not look first to fix themselves. To cultivate Tao, first you fix yourself.

Sometimes people need to sit there or stay in one place to fix themselves. For example, there are psychological victims of traumatic experiences who can only do something to maintain their physical, mental, and spiritual health without making a contribution to the world. Maintaining their health is already a great accomplishment for them. They have my sympathy. Others, however, courageously face their situation and choose to learn how to manifest positiveness out of a negative situation or low cycle in their life, and while so doing, share their experience so that others might also learn. They have my respect. [36:120]

Energy in Daily Life

People tend to think that the events of their lives are determined by external influences. They may blame their happiness or misfortune on a divine but external authority who arbitrarily imposes punishments and rewards upon them. Or they blame their mothers and fathers for either spoiling them or denying them the fulfillment of their early emotional needs. Perhaps they think it is their environment which is supportive or hostile toward them, or their racial or educational background which determines the joy or sorrow which enters their lives. Or maybe they feel that their lives are governed by blind chance. Generally, people tend to look no further than the superficial elements which compose their experience. They fail to realize the deep truth that what appears as external reality is actually only a mirror of their own inner consciousness.

It is the energy projected by an individual's own mind which creates his or her experience. Consciousness is the vessel. The events in one's life are merely the physical or mental manifestations of the vessel's contents. The events are thus nothing but reflected images of one's own mental energy. The secret to leading a positive life is to refine and harmonize one's energy so as to live in consonance with the order of the universe. Conversely, by holding negative energy in one's mind in the form of distorted thought patterns and attitudes, one's life will reflect negativity and disharmony.

Every facet of our being is a manifestation of energy. The human body is a complexly organized energy system comprised of physical materializations of the five phases of energy evolution. It is the vital energy, or Ch'i, which enables blood to circulate, glands to secrete, and metabolic processes to take place. The presence or absence of the heartbeat is the indication used to determine whether a person is alive or dead, but what is it that determines whether the heart beats or ceases to beat? The heart beats because the vital energy dwells within the body. If the vital energy leaves us, the body becomes like a dry, empty shell devoid of life. It is not our outer form upon which our lives depend, but rather it is the subtle Ch'i upon which our outer physical form depends.

Generally speaking, because energy is so subtle, we are not aware that it circulates in our bodies throughout our individual energy network. Yet the physical organism is tangible and therefore observable. The physical state functions as a mirror in which we can perceive the condition of the subtler states of being, those of mind and spirit. Most of us tend to take harmony and balance for granted because everything flows so smoothly without any particular distinguishing event to stand out and grab our attention or annoy us. However, when our energy becomes disordered and symptoms of disease begin to show, we become aware that there is a problem. If, for instance, a woman has an energy disorder such as emotional depression, the disorder may express itself in problems with her menstruation. She may have cramps or headaches or her period may arrive late or be totally absent. Although she is probably unaware of the subtle factors involved, she will recognize that something is wrong because her menstruation is a tangible, integral part of her life.

When the subtle Ch'i moves in the body, gross manifestations such as blood also move. Conversely, if the Ch'i becomes imbalanced or its movement is impeded, this will influence the balance of the glandular secretions as well as the circulation of the vital fluids in the body. There is an old proverb which states that "flowing water does not decay." This principle is equally true of energy. This is one of the fundamental principles of integral medicine and of the system of self-cultivation. When stagnation of energy and blood occurs and localizes, disease will appear. Cancer and ulcers are two of the many kinds of diseases which result from energy stagnation.

Engaging in strong emotion, either joy, sadness, or any other emotion, can create imbalance and blockage in the energy network, which in turn can cause the energy and blood in the related area to become stagnant or to explode in localized areas of the body. Emotion is a form of energy which creates the atmosphere in which our daily scenario takes place. When strong emotions arise in the mind, the peaceful order of one's energy circulation is disordered; tremendous energy is then generated in the body cavities, creating stress and pressure on internal organs. The heart and liver in particular are very fragile organs. They can become damaged easily from internal disorder and pressure caused by strong emotional excess. When a person becomes angry, the blood vessels of the head become congested. Should one of them be weak, it could rupture and bring on a stroke, or the negative energy which has risen to the head may be transformed into tears or obscene language. Emotional excess will damage the nerves and blood vessels, effecting poor blood circulation, imbalanced metabolism, and glandular dysfunction.

If, on the other hand, one's mental atmosphere is calm, healthy, and positive, it will allow the energy in the internal network to flow normally and unimpeded. The practical value of keeping the mind quiet and poised is that in this way there is no undue emotional force to create stress and disorder in either the internal or external environment.

By practicing self-cultivation techniques, one develops a sensitivity to the energies constantly circling within the body. Descending downward from the top of the head is the frontal general yin channel called the *jen mo*. The energy swirls down the *jen mo*, then returns up the back of the body to the head by way of the general yang channel, the *tu mo*. Like water, the natural tendency of the gross yin energy within the body is to flow downward. If this internal energy leaks away through elimination or sex, or through what is produced and consumed, then the life is kept accelerating and speeding. Then the health of the life is in danger if balance and self-discipline are not of personal concern. When the internal energy is controlled, like water being dammed, then it is guided through the energy channel like an aqueduct fulfilling the process of irrigation. The internal energy will naturally function to support the head and the spirit. This is the cyclic movement of the internal Ch'i.

The strong drive in all living creatures to produce offspring is the result of the gross physical energy flowing downward into the reservoir of the sexual organs located at the lowest level of the body's trunk. The refined yang energy is said to be like fire, in that its natural tendency is to rise upward. After undergoing refinement, the energy travels across the perineum and ascends up the back to the head. The lips function as the upper gate between the yin and yang channels, with the anus functioning as the lower gate.

When a person is born into this world, yin and yang become distinguishable. The goal of spiritual cultivation is to restore the oneness of the yin and yang energies through unifying the *jen mo* and the *tu mo* once again to function as one whole and continuous channel in the body's energy system.

It is impossible to establish clarity and order in our being unless our internal energies are in a state of harmony and balance. By utilizing in our lives the same cosmic principles which assure the harmonious functioning of the universe itself, we can nurture our vital energy and establish the internal balance necessary for a happy life. The principles treasured by ancient and modern sages are simplicity, equilibrium, harmony, and quietude. These principles display the practical value of allowing one's energy to evolve and function normally. By personifying these cosmic principles, we come to realize that we embody the entire universe. Microcosm and macrocosm become one.

The *Tao Teh Ching* tells us that man follows the Way of Earth. Earth follows the Way of all heavenly bodies, all heavenly bodies follow the Way of the eternal Tao, and the Tao follows its own nature. This is the principle of universal order, the nature of the cosmos whose perpetual rhythm is followed by all existence. Whether it be a single atom, the human body, or the body of the entire cosmos, all energy movement is essentially the same, always following the same principles.

Differences among living beings arise as a result of the degree of completeness of their energy systems. For example, the energy systems of creatures lower than humans on the evolutionary scale are generally more yin or more gross. Their degree of yang, or more subtle, energy is relatively low. Human beings hold the highest position in the earthly evolutionary scale because they embody a balance of both yin and yang energies, both physical and spiritual, gross and refined. Because it is potentially complete and balanced, the energy network in the human being is like that of the entire universe. Actually the internal channel system in the human body almost precisely mirrors the energy network of the universe.

It is only because we violate the natural equilibrium of the energy network of our being that we require self-cultivation as a remedy to bring us back to our integral state of evenness and balance. Most people develop only the physical aspect of their being and neglect the spiritual because the pressures of living in society turn their attention away from the subtle truths of life. Thus their lives manifest imbalance and disharmony. The purpose of the esoteric process of the Integral Way is to refine the gross physical energy to the more subtle level of spiritual energy so that we may once again connect our being with the Subtle Origin of the universe. This is sometimes called embodying or realizing the universe within your body. It is not just an idea or a theory, but has actually been experienced by generation after generation of achieved ones.

The eternal Tao is the primal energy of the universe. If one engages in following this energy by embracing Tao and acting only as an expression of Tao, one can become integrated with the essence of all life. Then, as the *Tao Teh Ching* puts it: "Without going outside the door, one understands all that takes place under the sky. Without looking through the window, one sees the Way." [38:24–29]

Achieving Harmony Internally and Externally

External influences consist of our immediate environment and celestial influences. Our immediate environment is our family, friends, and co-workers, our society, and our geographical location. As we grow up, we are subjected to emotional influences and mental conditioning, and all the problems inherent in the environment in which our socialization takes place. Our behavior is determined by the pressure and stress in our environment, and we are compelled to actions which we would not take under normal circumstances. With emotional balance and mental clarity, one can react directly even in the most difficult situations and can follow the universal nature of productiveness and creativity rather than indulge in destructive tendencies. If we allow external influences to intrude into our being, we lose our personal gravity, and as a result, our energy floats upward and we cannot remain grounded and centered in our three tan-t'ien [energy centers between the eyes, in the center of the chest, and between the kidneys, in the center of the body]. Then we will take actions which are beyond our normal measure, and problems and accidents will be unavoidable.

When one's energy is balanced and one's mind clear, then one's will is resolute. Conversely, if one's energy is unbalanced, one is easily manipulated by someone with negative energy or through one's own unclear mind. One is therefore moved to act without real desire and even against one's conscience and wisdom and one becomes dominated by unconscious psychological imitation. This tendency is exploited commercially and politically, especially through the media, and it is also found in religious emotionalism and educational approaches.

The sun is the most consequential of the celestial influences because it is the earth's major source of energy. It supports life on earth and determines the growth, the strength, and the daily energy cycles of all life. The energy of the moon, which follows a very distinguishable cycle of waxing and waning, plays a significant role in our intellectual and emotional life, and influences sexual desire and women's menstruation as well as the ocean tides. The full moon may cause restlessness and impulsiveness, but can also make people very energetic. It is a good time for cultivation and creative expression.

These natural universal influences reflect on our complex and stressful contemporary lifestyle. By developing sensitivity to celestial influences, we can adjust our lives to be in harmony with nature. Through the understanding of both our own and universal energy cycles, we can harmonize our internal energies with the universal energies. Integral cosmology is a topic dealing with specific knowledge and techniques related to universal energies.

The elements which influence us internally are our mind, our desires, and our impulses. The human mind can be an instrument of insight, inspiration, and ingenuity, and can assist us in our self-development and self-discovery, but it can also be our greatest enemy. Our beliefs and values bind our mind to the realm of dualistic vision. The original nature of the human mind, however, is absolute. The questions of good or bad and right or wrong are merely a creation of the dualistic mind.

Only one energy exists in the absolute realm, but in the relative realm it can manifest appropriately or inappropriately. This distinction lies still within the realm of pure morality. When this distinction is complicated through artificial concepts about behavior, it then becomes ordinary morality and may become an obstacle to the experience of life. For example, when a man marries a woman, it is appropriate behavior and a question of pure morality. But when their marriage is determined or prevented by religious denomination or social discrimination, then it is a question of ordinary morality. Mental conditioning and concepts will prevent one's spontaneous and harmonious expression and divert one's energy to manifest as internal emotional pressures.

Using the mind resembles using a camera. If one can achieve absolute oneness with what appears as the multiformity of the world, one can unify the fragments of one's mind and focus one's mental camera instantly to receive a clear and accurate picture of reality. This is the correct function of the mind.

Desire, an energy manifestation closely related to physical and mental energy, is frequently blamed as the cause for human problems. But trouble ensues only when desire is out of balance with the higher functions of the mind and serves the lower instead. The natural order is for the lower attributes of the mind to serve the higher, and for the mind to be the servant of the spirit or subtle energy which is the master over all aspects of a human being and all creation. The opposite order, however, predominates in most people's minds and is the reason for their problems and degeneration. Their minds are subdued by blind desire, which is a manifestation of physical energy.

When one's physical energy is overly strong in relation to one's mental energy and spiritual energy, one experiences difficulties in maintaining the equilibrium and harmony of one's being. Out of physical desire one may lose one's calmness and clarity of mind and be compelled to act against one's better judgment. Imbalance will also result when one's idealism is not in accord with the practical reality of one's life. The pursuit of mental as well as physical desire will disturb the equilibrium of the mind and prevent its effective and appropriate functioning.

The mechanics of desire are covert. A certain desire may not be fulfilled and may unconsciously trigger the activation of a different desire, and one may be motivated to satisfy an apparently inexplicable desire. Or one may not be equipped with the material means to satisfy one's desires and may therefore resort to inappropriate actions. When pure intelligence and wisdom rule one's mind, one's energy circulates smoothly throughout the body and subtle energy systems.

Impulse, which is also closely connected with the body and mind, is a strong motivating factor. It may be the direct response to a stimulus or may carry out the order indicated by desire. The quality of impulse is very sudden and immediate, and is therefore difficult to control. One tends to be impulsive especially when one's physical energy is unstable. Impulse can spring from any aspect of the mind and may be motivated by desires of physical or intellectual nature. In itself, impulse is neither positive nor negative. Difficulties arise only out of blind impulsiveness.

Blind impulsiveness is behavior which is involuntary, compelled by the needs and desires of the body and mind. If we follow our biological impulses to eat and procreate blindly, we will encounter many mishaps. Our hormonal secretions may stimulate the physical desire to procreate and the psychological suggestion to find a sexual partner, and we may neglect the importance of a spiritual connection with our partner; or this desire may be diverted to an abnormal desire for food or material possessions, or manifest as overexertion and other inappropriate behavior. When the expression of one's desire is guided by one's spirit, it is transformed into spontaneously correct and appropriate behavior and one is able to take full responsibility for the consequences of one's actions.

Spirit is the essence of our being. If spirit is the directing energy in our life, then our desires and impulses are balanced and harmonious and fulfill their natural function as expressions of the positive, creative, and constructive nature of the universe. In the absolute realm of spirit, the mind has the positive function of a highly sensitive transmitter and receiver, and is capable of spontaneous knowledge without previous experience of or the distinction between good or bad. Before one is able to receive spiritual enlightenment, one must be absolutely virtuous, practice the principle of appropriateness, and display one's innate moral qualities of selflessness and responsibleness. If one does not have the foundation of true and pure ethics, any spiritual teaching will be without influence on the reality of one's life. Spiritual knowledge and techniques alone may create mental stimulation, but are merely another form of LSD or mental opiate, and have nothing to do with the truth of spirit and the reality of life.

People generally believe that the mind is the place where they can enjoy freedom even in difficult situations. But this is a delusion. One attains freedom only through total liberation. Only the absolute mind is able to be a clear channel for the expansion of spiritual awareness and the experience of freedom. When we evolve beyond the realm of the dualistic and conditioned mind, then we will experience spiritual stability and live in harmony, simplicity and true freedom. This is the goal of integral self-cultivation. [38:104–108]

Gold from Sand

The "divine golden medicine" is the most important metaphor for the process of spiritual cultivation in the ancient tradition of integral spiritual development. Are you aware of how much gold can be gathered from tons of sand? In an ordinary life being, there may also be "gold"—the essence of life. Through the process of spiritual cultivation, one refines oneself, disposing of the sand and retaining the gold. Having obtained the gold, one then has the necessary material for refining the "divine immortal medicine."

Spiritual cultivation involves removing the coarse and keeping what is truly precious. This process involves a great deal of work. Many teachings emphasize throwing away what is coarse, but too often they throw away the essence at the same time. Some teachings even use that essence in exchange for what is false. These kinds of teachings are very popular in today's world. True cultivation requires much time and daily practice, whereas conceptual achievement can be immediate.

Hidden Gift

One important principle a Taoist teacher can give to his students in their practical life is to have courage and clarity of mind to try new things or face many kinds of life situations. Similarly, a person cannot always decide to refuse the many unpleasant, unhappy, or even harmful situations existing in life. The good outcome of any situation still depends on you; you can turn an unbeneficial situation around to be beneficial. If there is any secret of life, if there is any one game a Taoist likes to play in applying his life energy, it is not to work out his own created situation, but a situation given to him.

Once a student related her own experience to me. She referred to this principle as the "hidden gift." Any time this person had to accept unpleasant, boring, or less glamorous jobs, less-than-ideal living or sleeping situations, poor companionship or material insufficiency, and so on, she stayed with the situation and applied herself to it while looking for its hidden gift, which is the benefit in a difficulty. It was often some kind of learning about herself that made her understand life, herself, or others better. Sometimes it was acquiring proficiency or skill in order to make unpleasant jobs quite pleasant and fun to do. Sometimes it was material benefit, an unexpected opportunity, or a new friendship. Almost always there was also spiritual learning. Sometimes it was learning that she did not need to accept certain attitudes or kinds of treatment by other people any longer. It all depended on the situation that life gave to her in that moment. But there was always a benefit for her, as long as she stayed long enough and positively applied herself to the task. After she learned to do well with it, she would receive the benefit or learning. Difficulties lost their power over her because she knew there would always be a pleasant surprise hidden somewhere. I feel good about her achievement; thus, I quote her experience here. [21:25–26]

Cause and Effect

In general, things evolve from the subtle to the solid level, from the inside out, from the invisible to the visible, from the intangible to the tangible. What you do every day (in thought, desire, impulse, and emotion) forms you and makes you either more spiritually fit or unfit. You must therefore be spiritually responsible. There is no other choice. You must achieve yourself wisely and completely, not just partially. If you form yourself each day by thinking only of what you want and what you like, without considering the benefit of balance in all things, you will destroy the natural balance and organization of your soul by becoming extreme and partial. When you become more partial, you become more incomplete and crooked, contorting your original soul. When you enter worldly life again, you suffer and produce poison in yourself and your surroundings.

The main point in this is that all of you suffer from something; all of you have one shortcoming or another. The trouble is that you pay more attention to your suffering than to the rest of your life, thus aggravating the suffering. You don't know how to utilize what you have already achieved.

If you focused instead on the satisfaction of your present achievement and continued to cultivate yourself by doing good deeds, both for yourself and for others, this would be both a personal remedy and salvation as well as a way to mend your shortcomings and suffering.

For example, if you desire money only for yourself, you might undermine your health and be cruel to the people close to you. This would only take you further from the truth of life and from normalcy and completeness. The lives of prominent people can be the subject of much useful reflection.

Spiritually speaking, the defect that one creates by such imbalances affects not only one's present life but other lives as well, due to the constant needs and wants that result from spiritual imbalance. Someone who lives a good life and does good deeds is self-rewarded. Those who are greedy, covetous, and jealous of others are self-punished. In both Eastern and Western religions there is a hell. In ancient times, hell was taken very seriously; it was considered endless darkness, suffering and punishment for doing and being morally bad. Factually, hell is the experienced effect of one's actions lifetime after lifetime; it is simply the truth of the individual's life. The individual is a small universe that creates energy which manifests both internally and externally so that the person himself can actually become either heaven or hell. The whole of human society is made up of individuals who are developing themselves in one direction or another. New inventions, as well as social conflict, are the result of the direction in which a society develops as a whole. You need, therefore, to watch the cause, because the cause produces the effect.

At a practical level, say someone has a forked tongue and spreads scandal about someone else in a serious manner. Traditionally, according to the stories of some conventional religions, executioners in hell would put burning charcoal on the person's tongue. Although this was the old-fashioned way of moral education, the reality is that the person will doubtlessly punish himself with self-created problems that are not limited to the tongue.

What you suffer in your life today comes from two sources: a near cause (the result of doing things that have spiritually affected you) and a far cause (punishment from remote trouble in a past lifetime). As life continually forms itself, the spiritual effects of one's behavior will definitely emerge, either immediately or at a later time. Punishment and reward do not come from other people or from a divine authority. The unadorned reality is that they come from the way in which you have formed yourself.

People who kill other people must be killed themselves; killing invites killing. If you kill an innocent person, you will be killed for no reason. People should take responsibility for their society as well as for themselves. Today's world has reached a critical stage because of a lack of self-awareness and spiritual responsibility.

The facts gathered by spiritual pragmatism encourage people to attain spiritual self-awareness so that they can recognize the problems that they cause from day to day. As one develops by refining oneself daily, the problems of the past can be dissolved. Spiritual blessing and development are both attainable by continual spiritual discipline and cultivation. Your shortcomings and bad fortune are not reason to be discouraged. You are alive with creative energy. You can therefore reform yourself immediately through undaunted spiritual cultivation which will produce the self-awareness that can guide you toward spiritual completeness, abundance, and balance. [14:224–25]

The High Is Built by the Low

Sometimes you do better in life and other times you do poorly. When your cycle is high, you enjoy your life more than when you are having difficulties in a low cycle. To harmonize the flow of your life, do not become excited by the high points or depressed by the low ones. Always remember, the high is built by the low. You should respect the times when you are in a low cycle, the times when you are a nobody. Do not struggle to be somebody, because you will only be somebody when other people say you are somebody. "Somebody" is built on the moments when you are nobody. This guidance is not the same as ordinary teachings that only look for high respect and exaltation and do not value the low. When you look up to the high, spiritually and emotionally you are low. When you respect the low, spiritually and emotionally you are high.

When people have a low cycle, they think of it in an emotional way and feel terrible. They want to die or kill themselves. They feel boring, unattractive, and uninteresting. They receive no attention or respect from anyone, and they do not love themselves either. They do not realize that their low cycle can make them wise. Life is built up by each uninteresting moment, not just by excitement. Your destiny is that way too. [14:165]

Signs of Growth

We should recognize that low cycles are signs of further growth. At the same time, we should also recognize the potential for vitality or spiritual robbery when we experience different events and in our relationships. If your inner being does not remain calm and balanced, then your spiritual energy is robbed and your balance damaged. This can help a person of self-cultivation understand external circumstances better: utilize the circumstance to help your growth, but do not let it damage you.

I once lived in a place where two long rows of eucalyptus trees lined the walk to the house. Whenever the wind blew, the walk became covered with branches and leaves. This is like periodic disaster. People notice the loss of the branches and leaves, but they do not notice the trees constantly growing stronger. In your personal or business life, you sometimes suffer setbacks, but they may just be a sign of normal growth. So-called periodic disasters, like the falling leaves, are also signs of continuous growth. [42:113]

Sickness

The *Tao Teh Ching* says, . . . "The superior man knows what should be known by him. The sick one does not know what should be known by him. The one who is sick of being sick, therefore, can be free from being sick."

Sickness is caused by obstacles which must be over-come before you can reach for spiritual maturity. Here are Lao Tzu's guidelines to tell if you are sick or not.

To be moody and fussy and use others as your victim
is sick.

To be greedy and disregard righteousness is sick.

To be lascivious and ignore your own virtue is sick.

To cling to worldly objects is sick.

To hate others and pray for their death is sick.

To overindulge in something that you like and to
discard your spiritual light is sick.

To defame the reputations of others and then boast of
your own goodness is sick.

To change for your own benefit that which has already
been accepted is sick.

To rejoice in the misfortune of others is sick.

To convert your virtues to new, fashionable, immature
thoughts is sick.

To be in treacherous collusion is sick.

To pass rumors about anything is sick.

To hold a narrow view and mislead people is sick.

To make false statements is sick.

To defile the good name of others is sick.

To swindle simple people is sick.

To brag about your own achievements is sick.

To violently use your force, capability, and speech
is sick.

To be dualistic in thinking and unfaithful to your true
nature is sick.

To lie and cheat is sick.

To be meddlesome in the business of others is sick.

To disclose the secrets of others is sick.

To look into the activities of others without their
knowledge and approval is sick.

To bewilder people so that they will stumble and fall
is sick.

To teach evil is sick.

To rob people of their profits is sick.

To take from others when they do not have the strength
to resist is sick.

To be deceitful is sick.

To injure others with evil and crafty means is sick.

To postulate conclusions is sick.

To misappropriate and cheat is sick.

To suppress the weak and help the violent is sick.

To be hypocritical is sick.

To be untruthful in speech and insincere in thought
is sick.

To bend your own virtuous principles for popular
interests is sick.

To be jealous of another's virtues and capabilities
is sick.

To engage in extravagant talk and impure chatter
is sick.

To allure and entice the naive is sick.

To use slanderous language is sick.

To seduce the young, ignorant, or naive is sick.

To villify the virtuous is sick.

To exaggerate in emotions and speech is sick.

To radically treat those who are lost is sick.

To pride yourself on your own intelligence and to use
this sarcastically against others is sick.

To abuse your own influence by suppressing others
is sick.

To use force is sick.

To use social power to threaten others is sick.

To try to influence others with an alluring manner of
speech is sick.

To borrow and not return is sick.

To take pride in your wealth is sick.

To take pride in your honor and glory is sick.

To envy those who become prosperous is sick.

To ridicule the success of others is sick.

To please with, or be pleased by, flattery is sick.

To take pride in your own high virtue is sick.

To obstruct another from accomplishments is sick.

To disturb public affairs with selfish purposes is sick.

To disguise your bad motives with a beautiful approach
is sick.

To make people believe that you are straight when you
are actually crooked is sick.

To insult others with what you think is correct is sick.

To feel that others are disgusting but to praise yourself
is sick.

To think that you are superior to all others is sick.

To take credit for other people's accomplishments
is sick.

To complain about your own life is sick.

To make people believe that a fabricated story is true
is sick.

To endanger others in order to acquire or preserve your
own security, or because you like to behave this way,
is sick.

To incite a riot is sick.

To be critical of the affairs of others but not to practice
your own cultivation is sick.

To cause others to be burdensome is sick.

To take advantage of people is sick.

To use people's shortcomings as a means of controlling
them is sick.

To expect repayments for doing favors is sick.

To demand that people do you favors is sick.

To envy what others have acquired is sick.

To argue habitually is sick.

To curse animals is sick.

To use black magic is sick.

To disgrace the talents and virtues of others is sick.

To hate people or yourself because others are better
than you is sick.

To take drugs or use alcohol improperly is sick.

To hold prejudices is sick.

To not forgive others for their wrongdoings is sick.

To refuse the good advice and teachings of others
is sick.

To behave recklessly is sick.

To be unreasonable is sick.

To be self-righteous is sick.

To hold skepticism toward all truth is sick.

To make fun of people who are insane and ill is sick.

To be arrogant and impolite is sick.

To use vulgar and obscene language is sick.

To disrespect people who are young or old is sick.

To adhere to an unhealthy environment is sick.

To be undutiful in your work is sick.

To be irresponsible for your life is sick.

[8:80–83]

Sober and Tipsy

Spiritual soberness is retaining the ability to be attentive to and correctly responsive to one's environment, while
at the same time meeting the needs of one's higher life goals
(having a safe, healthy life being and providing a supportive

environment for one's spiritual practice and learning). This means, whenever you are at work, doing a good job; if at home, doing your share and keeping correct behavior; when in the marketplace, being attentive to accomplishing your tasks and alert to possible mistakes.

Spiritual soberness is a type of service to oneself and others. Spiritual traditions must agree that the path to Heaven is through service to others, because the constancy of working correctly can be a mirror to show a person how he is doing. If he loses his soberness, he knows it immediately because he sees errors arise in his work.

It is nice when you begin to see success in your cultivation of spiritual soberness. There are fewer errors in work and daily life, you begin to learn how to handle the ones that do come up, and you feel good about yourself and your life. People respond to you differently; maybe some of them stop trying to avoid you so much, because you have something to offer them. Also, some things bother you less or do not have the power over you that they did before. Your life has a greater feeling of richness, smoothness, and positiveness to it.

I believe that spiritual soberness is a good goal for many people. It is nice to describe it, but it is better to know how to start to achieve it. A person will achieve it by wanting it more than anything else. He just says to himself, "I want things to go well and right in my life at all times and in all situations," and then he begins to apply himself to seeing that it happens. Not just one day, but he reminds himself of his goal every day. Surely, no one can live a totally trouble-free life, but there is a certain point you reach where you know you are beginning to attain that goal of spiritual soberness and balance. Just do not give up, no matter what happens in your life.

Spiritual tipsiness is perhaps not as easy to understand as spiritual soberness.

Everybody in their life needs some enjoyment. There

are different kinds of enjoyment or "drunken feelings" possible in earth life. There are those brought by drugs or alcohol, those brought by illusions or religions, those brought by emotions such as extreme happiness or sadness, those brought by ownership of material possessions or certain relationships, those brought by accomplishing moral actions, and those that are purely spiritual. Whatever good feeling we reach is a kind of tipsiness or drunkenness. All are a movement of energy, but the difference between them is what energy is moved, how the energy is moved, and the amount of harm or harmlessness involved in moving it.

Spiritual tipsiness is the most excellent form of enjoyment because a person can do it and still maintain his soberness and harmlessness. That is, a person can still meet all his obligations and responsibilities; perhaps he even does better at them. Spiritual tipsiness is not harmful to others or oneself. However, it is important for people to learn the self-control and good lifestyle that are necessary to experience soberness and tipsiness at the same time if they want the full delight. Tipsiness alone is not enough. It is so much more wonderful to have one's life going well externally and also have the good feeling of spiritual tipsiness or contentment.

It is nice to describe spiritual tipsiness, but it is better to learn how to attain it in life. It is done through constantly practicing awareness of the center of the chest, or heart center, during all kinds of situations. For many people it is most easily experienced in quiet, alone times, but practicing it at all times, when suitable to do so, brings more result. This type of concentration moves the energy out of the intellectual head into the heart and creates the pleasant feeling. It is when a person stops thinking. Having a quiet or unstressful life makes it easier to do, because a person's energy is already somewhat more contained within his body rather than scattered out in confused or unnecessary events.

Spiritual soberness is when a person applies his life energy to making the world better. It is a movement of energy from the person's being out to the world. Spiritual tipsiness is when a person brings the energy back into his body to replenish himself. That makes it possible for him to continue to be around, work with, or serve other people in whatever way his life requires of him. It is the delightful movement of energy like the breath: in and out. When the two are balanced together, there is a perfection of being. I believe that a person who can attain both soberness and tipsiness at the same time is what they call the perfect person. That does not mean that all is perfect in his external life, but that he is perfectly balanced. [21:156–58]

Spiritual Tipsiness

Life, as it is, is sometimes boring, uncomfortable, or tedious, with lots of work and unpleasant environments, situations, or people. Hasn't that been your experience at times? So how do you handle living an ordinary, normal life amid the harsh world? You sometimes need a special thing. To support their being in the real world, some directly use alcohol or drugs, others turn to religious numbness, while some join a persecuting force to try to reorder or change the world. However, a Taoist uses a specially made wine that he brews from his wisdom. To be able to allow the world to be harsh, people to be cruel, and situations to push him, the effect of Taoist special wine might be the great virtuous fulfillment of forgiveness. He forgives the trouble, forgives the world, and forgives any people who wrong or mistreat him. Taoists do not call it forgiveness, however. Calling it forgiveness is a dualistic level and also makes one's ego too big; it puts the other people lower than you, so that they need you to forgive their error. It might be called "a Taoist's self-made tipsiness." This tipsiness and blurry vision keeps him from seeing the mistakes of others and the harm or loss to himself. He does not know how others have wronged him or how they have mistreated him. It is not that he does not see into it; he simply decides that he does not care about the small losses. He knows but he does not care. There is something much more interesting going on, and he can afford to take the loss anyway because he has built up his strength. He is such a wise and kind dummy. He does not push hostility to the extreme.

However, in practical life, some people feel pain or agony because they are too serious about every small thing. Sometimes, a person cannot be too critical or too clear about the details. The application of clarity or clear mind still requires a person's better management to know the right circumstance in which to apply it. So when one's spiritual tipsiness is applied to the right spot, it can be lubricating, useful, or helpful. At least it can make one's legs stronger; a person can stand stronger with it. All of this is to say that when you give people an easier time, it is also giving yourself an easier time. [21:162–63]

Benevolence

There was once a man, a sailor by profession, who was fond of sea gulls. Every morning he went into the ocean and swam about in their midst, at which times a hundred gulls and more would constantly flock about him. One day his father said to him: "I am told that the sea gulls swim about you in the water. I wish you would catch one or two for me to make pets of them." On the following day the sailor went to the ocean as usual. But lo! The gulls only wheeled about in the air and would not alight.

—Lieh Tzu

If the energy embodied by a person is harmonious, it will naturally express itself as benevolence toward all creation, and in response he or she will be treated with benevolence by all other beings and things. There is no need to create special occasions for being benevolent. The subtle energy responds most effectively when one's expression is spontaneous and within the course of ordinary life. Being benevolent only toward a particular person or motivated by one's own particular preference will be futile. The attempt to appease one's troubled conscience through charities will cause the appropriate negative response of subtle energy. According to the unfailing principle of subtle energy response, it is impossible to be hypocritical before the universal law.

Benevolence displays itself inconspicuously, naturally, and spontaneously, and causes positive and constructive responses. When a person is living and acting benevolently, his or her life will be a reflection of the inner harmonious energy. [38:129–30]

Gentleness

Enjoy gentleness instead of excitement. Many people learn to enjoy excitement. It starts when they are babies and their mother, father, and other relatives all excite them. They like to make the baby excited and happy. But that is a baby; when you grow you need to learn to enjoy gentleness instead of excitement. Excitement usually has a side effect; gentleness usually gives perfect happiness. Modern people enjoy motorcycles and so forth; a Taoist is wise enough to enjoy slowness instead of speediness. [36:94]

The Value of Boredom

Learn to enjoy boredom and monotony. When you feel bored, it means that it is a really good time and everything is in good condition. This is the most valuable time for you. Most people are unpleasant when things are boring, because they do not know the value of boredom and monotony. Monotony to them is too simple, and they cannot stand it. Those things you consider boring and monotonous can help you come back to yourself instead of pulling you away. By accepting them, you can nurture yourself. [36:94]

Which Would You Prefer?

Your time on this earth is like an oil lamp. Excitement is the flame and your life is the oil. The more excitement, the faster the oil is exhausted. Which would you prefer, to enjoy quickly or to enjoy longer? The spiritual enjoyment of a person is like having the light with a connection to the great source. It will never be exhausted. [42:142]

Fun

A student remarked: It seems that life is so hard. There is no fun or pleasure included in this, or any other, spiritual instruction you have given.

The teacher smiled and answered: Do you know what fun is? When one abides in naiveté and innocence, joy grows from within. When the mind becomes too complicated and sophisticated, simple fun can no longer be satisfying, then harmful fun is invented. To maintain naiveté and innocence is to truly enjoy life.

Personally, I do not look for fun. When fun comes, I enjoy it. If one looks for fun or creates fun it is not fun. It loses its quality from the extra labor. When fun comes by itself, alongside the main direction in your life, you enjoy it. Then you can include it as a part of your life. Besides that, life itself and work are fun, too. A healer helps sick people become well. A mechanic fixes whatever comes to his hand. Is that not fun? In everyday life, if you walk a couple of miles, or grow flowers or fruit in your backyard, is that not fun, too? Most healthy, creative activities are fun.

It is as the old master taught: life is complete and joyful. Beyond accomplishing the basic needs of your life, to look for achievement or excitement is an unnecessary addition to life. Thus, he teaches no extra doing in achieving your life. [35:121–22]

Guidance for Universal Good

Doing the following fortifies your spiritual glory and immortality:

March on the road where you are morally supported. Retreat from the entrance of evil.

Do not take the side paths which tell you to become successful faster.

Do not do in darkness what you think nobody knows.

Accumulate self-disciplines which can benefit yourself and others by exercising good will, but do not put it up for sale.

Be kind to all lives.

Be loyal to your good work.

Assist your parents and the elderly when they are in need.

Be friendly and kind to youngsters.

Straighten out your own life first before you teach others.

Have sympathy for the orphaned.

Help the helplessly widowed.

Protect those younger than yourself.

Do not hurt any insect, grass, bush, or tree without good reason.

Have pity for people's problems.

Be happy about other's achievements.

Help others in emergency.

Save people from danger.

View another's attainment as your own. Have compassion for another's loss as your own loss.

Do not make a show of others' shortcomings. Do not dazzle people with your own advantages.

Stop the spread of evil influence and assist the development of good.

It is a sign of spiritual growth when you can take what is less, not complain when you are humiliated, and be surprised by receiving a favor.

When you do a kindness for another, do not expect it to be returned.

Do not feel remorse when you have given something good to people.

By following these, one will prove to be an upright person. All people respect such a one. Heaven protects him. Blessings and enjoyment catch him. All evils keep away from him. All gods defend him. He will achieve what he wishes to accomplish. He is hopeful to attain spiritual glory and immortality.

One who aspires to attain a high level of spiritual achievement should follow a model of spiritual perfection. One who wishes to live a normal life with full spiritual potential should do his best to follow the above advice.

It is dangerous to one's spiritual life to be unrighteous and go against the moral nature of the universe, so the following should be thoroughly avoided:

Making evil your talent and cruelty your capability in action, to hurt others

Planning or participating in schemes that harm people

Doing things to damage the harmony of a nation or a family

Disrespecting the teacher who has nurtured your life spirit

Being disloyal to your duty

Cheating the undeveloped

Defaming your fellow students

Being hypocritical and treating others falsely
Trusting your strong-headedness and not being kind
Being arrogant and self-assertive
Being unreasonable, unjust, and unfair
Moving toward what is wrong and turning your back
    to what is right
Pursuing personal credit by oppressing those inferior
    to you
Flattering those above you to obtain special favor
Being ungrateful to those who help you
Bearing a strong resentment toward another
Giving no value or respect to other people's lives
Disturbing the order of the peace of the world
Encouraging the unrighteous
Punishing the innocent
Taking money for killing others
Taking position by pushing others away
Killing the surrendered and captured
Boycotting the upright and the virtuous
Suppressing minorities and the helpless
Taking bribes
Making the right wrong and the wrong right
Punishing a minor crime as though it were a big one
Determining someone's punishment when you are
    angry
Knowing about a personal mistake or bad habit but not
    correcting it
Knowing a good thing but not actualizing it in your
    own life
Excusing your own responsibility to another
Stopping the development of the good ways or
    practices that another has discovered or stopping
    another from developing himself
Spreading malicious rumors or verbally attacking the
    sages

Transgressing the natural moral law

Killing birds or animals, disturbing the hibernating, stopping up holes, upsetting nests, harming the conceived, or breaking eggs for no constructive reason

Wishing that other people have trouble

Destroying people's success

Telling others it is safe when your purpose is to endanger them

Benefiting yourself by decreasing what belongs to others

Exchanging the bad with the good

Using private reason to harm the public

Taking credit for another's achievement

Concealing another's goodness so that others will not know about it

Describing another's ugliness

Revealing people's private lives

Consuming other people's goods

Separating people's close relationships

Taking what other people love away from them

Helping others do bad

Relying on superior brute force

Looking for an upper hand by humiliating others

Destroying other people's efforts

Damaging a person's marriage

Being proud of your own wealth

Failing to face your own conscience

Taking the credit belonging to another but refusing to take responsibility

Escaping responsibility by shifting the blame for an incident onto another person

Being motivated by the promise of fame and social recognition

Concealing another's or your own dangerous schemes

Diminishing another's achievement
Protecting your own shortcomings
Relying on your power to threaten people
Encouraging killing
Wasting food
Encouraging or requiring people to join in war or
    making them participate in meaningless labor
Destroying people's houses and taking their goods
Setting fire or damaging dikes with the intent of
    harming people
Destroying another's plans and undertakings in order
    to ruin their success
Destroying others' tools in order to make them unable
    to accomplish what is necessary
Wishing that people fall when you see their glory
Wishing that people lose their fortune when you see
    them become rich
Wishing to touch a person whose beauty you admire
Wishing that others die because you are indebted to
    them
Hating a person because he does not give you what you
    ask for
When you see another's accident, deciding it must be
    his own fault
Laughing at a person because he is crippled
Frustrating a person who is more talented than you by
    blocking a good opportunity for him
Forcing people to give you what you want
Being violent and aggressive in life
Indulging in pleasures of the flesh
Being unfair in your treatment of others
Ill-treating those who are subordinate to you
Threatening others
Complaining
Borrowing but not returning

Asking for extra payment
Using another's strength to actualize your own
    personal expansion
Appearing kindly but having a poisonous mind
Teaching incorrect or untruthful material
Enjoying bragging
Becoming jealous often
Extending preference to others

The following things do not harm other people, but they violate your own spiritual energy, especially in a natural environment.

Cursing the wind and rain
Walking over an outdoor well used to obtain drinking
    water
Stepping over cooking tools and materials
Walking over food
Jumping over another person's body
Having an abortion
Having peculiar habits
Making merry in the day and night of no moon, and at
    the end of a season (each period of seasonal
    transition)
Being angry at the beginning of the new moon or in the
    morning
Facing north when doing your elimination outdoors
Singing or crying while facing the oven and when
    cooking
Cooking food over a stove heated with dirty firewood
Getting up in the nude at night to urinate
Killing or hunting during the seasonal points of the
    equinoxes and solstices
Spitting at shooting stars
Disrespecting the natural sources of all light, the sun,
    the moon, and the stars

Using a fire during spring hunting
Cursing while facing north
Suffering bodily exhaustion
Indulging in excessive anger
Indulging in a drunken spree, small or large
Experiencing excessive sorrow
Holding hatred
Living in fear
Overly starving yourself
Overeating or eating food that is too cold, too hard, or
    too hot
Overindulging in sex
Becoming startled
Being imbalanced between working hard and doing
    nothing
Keeping your body too hot or too cold
Maintaining an irregular living schedule
Thinking too much
Talking too much
Sleeping too much

[36:46–51]

Emotional Balance

When unaware of the subtle influences which affect
your moods, it is easy to become dominated by the emotions.
Then you tend to identify completely with emotions, and they
are no longer just one component of life. This reveals itself in
statements such as "I am happy," "I am sad," and so forth.
By identifying with emotions, you are unable to spontaneously respond with the appropriate normal expression in the

arising situations. In this way, your whole being is molded by the emotional aspect of your energy structure.

If people are unaware of their emotional imbalance, they may content themselves with mental consolations such as "I am entitled to feel however I feel. This is the way I am." Or they may fall into the opposite extreme and forcefully suppress their emotions, denying the positive and healthy function of their feelings and normal reactions. This violates their true nature and occurs frequently in traditions which practice asceticism.

As long as one is unaware of the possibility of evolving beyond a trying emotional life, one will either deny one's healthy emotional expression or constantly struggle with emotional ups and downs. In either case, one usually experiences repeated defeats.

A positive approach to emotional life is the conscious guiding and directing of one's internal energy. In order to transcend the emotional approach to life, we have to conduct our energy consciously and appropriately. Through the practice of meditation one may accomplish the continuous circulation of one's internal energy and, as a consequence, experience a calm mind and a profound change in one's emotions and reactions to life. With a peaceful and clear mind, we can recognize that most of our emotional disturbances occur without any real reason. An emotional disorder may be stimulated by something of little or no importance. But in order to justify an emotional upset, we may unconsciously exaggerate and dramatize any small incident and transform it into a severe problem.

It is helpful to observe one's own emotional reactions with a clear and centered mind because they reflect the state of one's physical and mental energy. A person with balanced energy will manifest appropriate and harmonious emotional reactions.

The healthy emotional expression of a human being has

two primary elements which are a sign of natural self-discipline: the innate qualities of self-control and self-respect. Both these attributes are rooted in serenity. Serenity unfolds itself as a calm inner happiness, and it is enduring and completely independent of external conditions. Self-control and self-respect combined manifest as the ability to be conscious of, or sensitive to, transgressions toward oneself and other human beings as well as toward all creation. These fundamental and innate qualities of our nature need to be cultivated continuously for us to remain unaffected by artificial or environmental influences.

Ordinary happiness expresses itself as a release of emotional tension, and is really a dissipation of energy. One actually expends energy with the outburst of happiness. If experiences follow which can be interpreted as negative, this increases our susceptibility to being overwhelmed. Ordinary happiness is only a momentary and occasional experience.

Self-respect in the ordinary sense is based on the self-esteem derived from accomplishments, social status, and other external criteria. It is combined with rigidity and dogma, and depends on the evaluation of someone external to oneself. Ordinary self-respect denies the need to release our internal emotional pressures and stiffens our natural capability to be sensitive to infringements in our relationships and in our environment.

Integral self-cultivation employs certain methods for the restitution of one's natural emotional quality of serenity. Deep meditation and reflection lead us to self-discovery, and the practice of "self-release" gives us the experience of absolute oneness.* Both release the tensions we have accumulated in the past and free us from worries about the future. The practice of these methods will gradually dissolve all obstructions in our energy flow. At the same time, we extend our

---

*See Master Ni's book *Internal Alchemy* for information about this exercise.

being into the subtle universal realms and reach profound awareness. We connect our being with the whole continuum of time and space in an absolute way.

Absolute happiness and healthy sensitivity can be realized only through true self-discovery and through self-release. It is important, however, to refrain from any ambition in self-cultivation, as it will have detrimental effects. Only self-control and self-respect further spiritual evolution. If we combine sincerity with self-control, we will stay free from entanglement in worldly and spiritual illusions. Likewise, sincerity combined with self-respect will guide our emotions appropriately.

As a result we will reach true self-awareness and mastery over dissipation. Respect creates receptivity to higher frequencies of energy and can raise one from the ordinary relative realm to the absolute realm of existence. If one strives for happiness alone, one inevitably falls into moral depravity and loses one's well-being. By restoring and invigorating the natural awareness in the heart of our being, we transform life into a sacred expression of our unity with all aspects of the universe. Unity and harmony characterize the way we experience reality when we adhere to our innate qualities of self-discipline or self-control. Then we respect our own being and neither violate nor scatter our physical, emotional, mental, and spiritual energies, whether we are alone or in the company of others. [38:93–95]

Are You the Person?

Perhaps many people have given you trouble. Perhaps you have difficulty communicating with some people. Many people make you feel uncomfortable. Many people make you cautious. Many people make you nervous. Many people make you nauseous. Many people make you wish not to see them anymore. That is all acceptable.

Are you the person making other people feel they have difficulty to talk to you? Are you the person who makes others feel uncomfortable? Are you the person who makes waves all the time? Are you the person who makes others feel nauseous? Are you the person who makes people not want to see you anymore? You need to brighten your dark spots if you have any. No matter where you are, always be with your Heavenly energy manifesting as love, care, help, friendliness, or at least be at peace.

You might ask, how can we express our Heavenly energy under difficulty? You do not need to do anything. You can be an ordinary, common person. You may be unnoticed. Just do not be harmful. If in a situation where you can help, give help. If you cannot, do not force yourself. Help yourself first. Take care of yourself first. Take care of your health, take care of whatever you need, but do not pull other people down, squeeze people, press people, or strip people so that you will feel temporarily better. [22:33–34]

Overcome Obstacles

The spiritually developed ones suggested that we get rid of obstacles. If you overcome the obstacles in your life, then you attain the Way. Basically, you don't need to do anything right, you only need to avoid doing anything wrong. That in itself is doing things right.

There are a number of things that those spiritually achieved ones considered as obstacles:

The first obstacle is the troubled feeling that comes from needing to make a living. This doesn't mean you abandon making a living; just learn to support yourself without trouble.

The second obstacle is the interference of influential elders or loved ones.

The third obstacle is emotional entanglement with family members or friends. They can become obstacles for learning and being with the Way.

The fourth obstacle is the bondage of fame and profit that prevent you from being with the Way.

The fifth obstacle is having troubles, problems, and disasters that fill your life and distract you from being able to cultivate the Way.

The sixth obstacle includes customs, improper disciplines, and conventional social demands, which make you unable to live naturally and be yourself.

The seventh obstacle is the many ideologies that try to influence you and pull you away. Practically, they are only products, not the substance of life.

The eight obstacle is laziness.

The ninth obstacle is apathy, which allows you to pass the time away, day after day, year after year, without achieving yourself.

These nine obstacles prevent people from achieving the Way. If you are determined to strengthen the deep spiritual center of your life, then don't accept anything that is an obstacle, or, if it is unavoidable, limit its influence in your life; don't allow it to stunt your spiritual growth. You can still attain the Way by transforming the obstacle into a supportive factor. A spiritual life is the prize of those who win through harmony rather than war. [26:24–25]

Reading

In a wool sweater, once you find the end of the one piece of yarn, if you have the patience you can unravel the whole sweater safely, with no damage to the wool, and make a better one. Spiritual achievement is something like that, if you can find the end of the wool thread of the sweater. Do not waste time in irrelevant searches that do not come directly to the point or any books whose authors have never really experienced what they wrote about; by doing so you will use your energy to become a bookworm and have the achievement of a bookworm. However, you have to do some reading. If you do it with the goal of attaining development or immortality, then the whole blockage will unravel for you and the breakthrough will be achieved. It is an internal thing, not an external thing. It is as though the firewood is there, but you need a match to start the fire. One small match, that is all. The material comes from you, the realities you have been through in many lifetimes. [42:275]

Four Things to Avoid

A spiritually developed one does not hold personal opinions, insist that something must be done, insist on the way something is to be done, or persist in doing things his way. In other words, the four things he avoids are: "It must be me," "It is a must," "It is necessary," and "It is absolutely true," when he applies his mind to general activities. [35:48]

Ten Worthy Goals

If there are any truly valuable commandments in life, they are the following goals worthy to attain:

1. Mellowness of mind

2. A healthy, balanced life

3. An unobstructed, undefeated spirit

4. Loving people and rendering service

5. Unifying the body and mind

6. The rich emotion of enjoying simple relationships and things

7. Frequent self-examination of one's personal and public life

8. Avoidance of obsession and extravagance

9. Humility

10. Constantly collecting the floating emotions that take you out of your center

[14:108]

Some Conditions of Longevity

- Be a good person. No bad person can live long.

- Carry no conscious burden. This means do not owe anything to anyone. This means that you have not done anything wrong to people. If you have done something wrong,
straighten it out. Take care of all your old problems. I believe correct virtuous fulfillment can remove a conscious
burden.

- Have a reasonable philosophy which affects your psychol-
ogy. This means have a reasonable view of life that is not
overly emotional. No one who enjoys melancholy can live
to be very old. Have lots of laughter instead of angry yell-
ing. Also, never develop a philosophy of self-pity. You do
not need to be an aggressive person to show that you are
strong. Just be reasonable; do not be either too pessimistic
or too optimistic.

- Learn from the right teacher. The *Tao Teh Ching* teaches
longevity, especially the *Esoteric Tao Teh Ching*.
   Lao Tzu himself lived to be 260 years old. The Yellow
Emperor visited the mountains and learned from Guang
Ching Chur, who at that time was 1,200 years old. Another
teacher, Tien Chen Huang Lin, was already 3,000 years old
when the Yellow Emperor visited him. When you look at
the ancient record, although it could not be considered gen-
uine history, know that it carries a certain truth. The ancient record said that Pang Gu physically lived to be over
30,000 years old while he was ruling the earth. Then came
Tien Huang Shr (the Emperor of Heaven), Ti Huang Shr

(the Emperor of Earth), and Tung Huang Shr (the Emperor of People), each of whom lived to be over 10,000 years old. Then, slowly, the physical human body became smaller. It was no longer as gigantic as that of the early people. The lives of people were also shortened.

You may wonder if I seriously accept the ages described above. Those ages were listed in the ancient records. True or not, it has been proven that people can live to a ripe old age if they are still strong and active. The ones who lived to be 10,000 years old were more spiritualized than people who only lived to be 120 years old. . . .

• A young elephant will live to be very old because the mother elephant lived to be very old. If a person's ancestors were short-lived, then that person's own life will be limited by that foundation. Thus, your personal genes carried from your parents are one factor of your longevity. Although you are very much conditioned by the genes you carry, if you learn the health sciences provided by this tradition and apply them correctly, you should outlive any limitation you receive.

• Physical longevity has limitations unless you learn correct spiritual practice that uses your spiritual potential to lengthen your physical potence. This is a key point of the spiritual science of longevity.

• A good diet is important. Eating lots of animal meat with red blood is not considered healthy. All animal food is conditioned by the health of the animal, thus I believe that you need to be very selective in that category and eat only small quantities of healthy meats. In order to spiritualize yourself, your diet should not have more than 10 to 15 percent meat in your daily consumption. (You can obtain information about diet from the *Tao of Nutrition*, written by Maoshing Ni.)

- In general, you can use some herbal supplements. This is one of the practices of using the earthly source, which can help you have better energy and a stronger immune system.

- If you have a minor ailment, then you can utilize natural remedies such as herbal medicine or acupuncture, which create no side effects and leave no toxins in your body, which might take years to dissolve or disappear.

- It is important to have correct sexual attitudes. Some people who live to be very old are still very sexy, and are just as strong as young people. None of them are homosexual. Anything which is unnatural must have defects. Therefore, I do not recommend homosexuality as a practice, although it can be recognized as a circumstantial fact to people who do not find companionship with the opposite sex.

  Correct sexual practice is also very important. If you are celibate, it should be artful, which means that you transfer the sexual energy to be higher energy. However, the rigid practice of celibacy is not realistic. If you have a sexual partner, you still need to respect the physical and emotional cycles of both yourself and the other person. It does not mean you can have as much sex as you wish just because you have a partner. Having the right partner and sharing sex at a time good for both of you helps you both. It is not as harmful as the use of sex for physical or emotional release of tension.

- Your job and living environment are direct factors which determine your health. That knowledge is not special; it is common sense, but I would like you to look at it. Take the healthiest job you can unless you consider that your work has special spiritual meaning or you have a personal dedication to it. For example, to be a doctor or nurse is not the healthiest job, because every day you contact sick patients, but it is spiritually meaningful.

- The type of clothing you wear is also important. Tight or thick clothing is not as good as clothing which is a little loose and light. Natural fabrics are preferred over synthetics. However, having expensive clothing is not the goal of a spiritual life. Simple, clean, inexpensive, and natural are general principles for healthy clothing.

- In modern life, living accommodations are very different from the ancient style of life. We cannot be too particular or picky about every detail. The evil of pickiness or quibbling will cause you a lot of inconvenience as well as difficulty adapting to the new time. All of us need to lower our standard to meet some external conditions to avoid creating fear inside of us.

- Fear can kill people. Sometimes the danger of a reality is less damaging than the fear caused. Once I heard a story about three brave young men who lived in a village. They heard that there was a monster in a mountain cave who occasionally appeared on the roadside and frightened people. The three brave young men decided to finish the monster by going to fight with it. They took their weapons and went to the mountain to look for it. They kept searching until at last they came to a spot which had a very scary feeling. They heard a noise which became louder and louder, and then they saw a shadow. All of these were signs that the monster was coming. Two of them decided to run away, but the other one stood there, motionlessly, with apparent great courage. The two young men who ran to hide expected that their friend would join them soon afterward, but he did not.

  While the two young men were waiting in their safe spot, they both thought about how their friend had so much more courage than they did to face the danger of the monster. One of them thought about how the village would choose to make him their leader. The other young fellow was prepared to convince his parents to marry his sister to the brave young man. They kept waiting, but their friend did not join them. However, after a long time, all sounds disappeared and everything returned to normal, with the strong afternoon sun shining above them.

They were impatient to see their friend's victory. They slowly approached the original spot where the young man was. They approached, calling to him, but received no response. Finally they saw him. He was very weak and pale, so they believed that he was exhausted from the fight, although they did not actually see any signs of a struggle. It was their responsibility to carry the young man down to the village, where he received very good care because he was accepted as the hero who overcame the monster.

It took two months for him to recover. Finally, his friends went to hear about his experience of fighting the monster. First they expressed their admiration. Then they said, "When we heard the noise and felt the cold wind in the trees, we knew it was coming. We were afraid; we started to run involuntarily. We expected you to run with us, but you did not. We truly admire your courage for having conquered the monster. Please tell us how you fought it. The village is ready to give you a big reception. My sister, the most beautiful girl in town, is going to marry you. Please tell us what you did."

The young man told them simply, "I was not brave. I was stricken by fear, and my muscles were paralyzed, so I could not move. Both of you had the strength to run away, but I could not."

Then the two friends said, "We don't believe it. Then how did you fight the monster?"

The young man said, "There is no monster. At least I did not see it. You know what: the noise, the scary feeling, the cold air, and the shadow of the trees were just part of our fear. I have reflected on this during the last two months that I have been lying here being cared for by the good heart of all of you."

The two young men decided to cover up the fact that there was no monster, because they shared part of the glory. Thus, the hero was married to a beautiful girl and recognized as the most powerful man in the village.

This next story describes how fear can affect normal people. During World War II, Japanese airplanes came to bomb my hometown. At first, the people in our town were not afraid because they did not know what the bombs could do. After they experienced the first bombing, fear was at a very high level whenever the air raid sirens sounded. The fear caused a tremendous psychological effect. People had different physical reactions to the sound of the sirens, such as needing to use the toilet or stomachs having spasms. Thus some people developed ulcers.

• Choose an agreeable life companion. I mean, basically find agreement with each other, although there will be small conflicts all the time or just the process of understanding each other and coming to agreement. Small conflicts are basically unimportant and can be easily resolved if you are just a good companion. If there is no big problem between you and your companion, the harmony and peace you share can bring a good condition for achieving longevity. Harmony in a family is a good foundation to keep from having ulcers. Ulcers are not only caused by nervous work conditions, but also by a nervous family life.

• Learn to do simple art, housework, or anything by hand. When you do things by hand, your mind can relax. That is important. In general circumstances, your handwork can help reduce your meaningless nervousness or anxiety and keep your negativity from playing on you.

- Try to avoid negativity, worry, and anxiety.

- If you wish to follow a semifocused practice of mind, there are a number of invocations in the *Workbook for Spiritual Development of All People.* You can choose one or several of them and recite them by memory. It can be done any time. You can do it to protect your mind from scatteredness and from being pulled away by certain attractions. It is especially good to do this to start your morning, and in the evening, when you need to gather this part of energy in your life without allowing your mind to wander among external things.

- Do not allow dullness or boredom in life to cause your energy to become stagnant. Keep active by doing all kinds of healthy movement such as walking, simple Ch'i Kung (Qi Gong), Eight Treasures, Dao-in, and so forth. In addition, gardening or any gentle, relaxing handicraft is also beneficial.

- Financial stability is also important. There is no need to become too rich, but still have a stable source of being.

- A stable lifestyle includes having a healthy schedule, such as rising early and not going to sleep too late.

- Having fun does not mean you make fun of people or make fun of yourself. It means you have the capability to accept any severity or any costly or unmanageable situation of life. You always can find fun in it and make it part of your nutrition instead of trouble which can pull you down.

  This means you need to work on your sense of humor to see you through life difficulties or relationship difficulties rather than experiencing them as opportunities for bitterness.

- Try to enjoy every moment of your life and find great expansion in each moment. Do not make your whole life journey an unpleasant trip. Life connects not only with your attitudes, but also with treating life as an art. You can find something very interesting in each moment, even when it is most uninteresting to other people.

- No life can stop moving ahead. Nobody can be attached to the shape of physical life. The ancient wise ones deeply understood the ambition of living forever physically, but they knew that physical life is not reliable. They discovered that a higher level of life could be attained by following nature and working on their spiritual evolution to grow spirits. This was done by using the foundation of physical life.

  It does not matter what age you are now; you can contemplate which way to go. One way is the way of the ancient achieved ones that continues the possible evolution of your present life. Another way is to bet on the physical life. Usually the result of that is to overserve the physical life; what happens then is you will grow no spiritual essence and rely on the mechanical approach of modern medicine. Modern medicine cannot give you any hope for lengthening your enjoyable physical existence. The way of modern medicine would destroy a spiritual future.

- Truthfully speaking, longevity is a side effect of spiritual cultivation. Spiritual cultivation is different from following a religion. Those who are responsible for their own lives— spiritually, mentally, and physically—have no thought of depending upon any external force. The realistic achievement of longevity is attained step by step, as I have revealed in my different books. If you follow the instructions in the books, you can build more spiritual confidence by finding the proof of spirit and then knowing the possibility of spiritual life.

  When your goal is spiritual immortality and you make every effort to support this direction, your achievement of longevity is more possible than for people who are only attached to the physical shape of life.

- During the process of spiritual cultivation, do not use strong toxic medication or overapply surgery as the main assistance of your life. Instead, you need to continue your spiritual effort to maintain yourself in one piece. To a spiritual person, the shape of physical life is like a raft you utilize to cross the rough water. Once you are across the rough water, I think you greatly enjoy your freedom on the dry land and do not need to carry the raft on your back. This is just advice for serious spiritual preparation rather than expecting a long physical life which has no meaning.

- Many martial arts champions did not last long, yet if you do martial arts correctly, they support your health and strength. Because their intention is warlike, the gentle type of martial arts better serves your health and life strength. Their original shape was Dao-in and Ch'i Kung. These serve your health the most.

- In general, movement arts and quiet sitting meditation each have a different function to assist your health. Alternating application of them was set up and passed down by the ancients. Alternating these practices is of greater benefit than the single practice of one or the other.

- My father told me that there are three things which need to be fulfilled in order to achieve longevity or immortality. One is to keep your physical body complete without doing anything to damage it or allowing it to be damaged by any type of tyrannical social system or government.

  The second is to keep your personal, natural virtue complete. This means to keep your heart whole without being damaged. In other words, maintain your conscience in perfect condition without doing anything to shame yourself or damage your natural virtue as a dignified human being.

The third is to maintain the natural allotment of years in your life. It seems that each individual has a natural length of life. Each individual needs to do his or her best to reach the end of the natural allotment without losing life in the middle or by suffering a negative effect from the external environment.

These three fundamental things underlie the teaching of the Integral Way and connect with all good spiritual practices. My father was a great model who was still able to fulfill at least these things even while living under the difficulty of a communist regime. For details, see *Eternal Light*.

• Learn from the spiritual truth. In the world, the example of the highest immortality is Tao, the Subtle Origin. There are two categories of existence: one is beingness and the other is nonbeingness. All beingness is subject to change or subject to final extinction. Even the concept of God is in the category of beingness. The only thing which is not subject to change or extinction is the nonbeingness of the spiritual origin. Thus, the highest immortality cannot be counted by numbers. That nonbeingness is true immortality, the Tao Body, the body of truth, or the life of Tao.

A student of the Integral Way does not make any one person or being the sole example of immortality, but prepares himself or herself step by step to live the Body of Tao. That is the highest achievement of immortality.

The meaning of immortal practice is to destroy your attachment to physical life, although you still respect it. The conceptual inflexibility of believing that the body is your life causes strain for your mind and brings no benefit to your long, healthy, happy life. [29:145–155]

Love

The mutual response of two young hearts presents the picture of love. In the *I Ching* this is illustrated by a young girl, and a young boy, and the mutual attraction shared between them.

When I was young, I focused more on my spiritual achievement than on experiences of love. After studying the important teachings of the three main cultural traditions— Taoism, Confucianism, and Buddhism—I harmonized and expressed all three with the following words:

> Confucianism is my garment,
> Buddhism is my cane,
> and Taoism is my sandal.

My young, proud mind seemed to be satisfied with this combination. However, one day I discovered that someone had added some new, handwritten words to each line of my writing on the wall of my study. These lines now said:

> Confucianism is my garment,
> —it is too short for you!
> Buddhism is my cane,
> —it is too weak to support you!
> and Taoism is my sandal
> —it has been worn out long ago!

My first response to this discovery was outrage. I thought it must be my younger brother or elder sister making fun of me, but since it did not seem to be an ordinary joke, I immediately corrected my judgment. The person who wrote these lines had to have a vision higher than, or equal to, mine.

I felt puzzled. Who could have done this? Since the handwriting was not much better than mine, it could not be the work of a dignified adult. Also, this happened to be my personal study upstairs. I was the only one who used most of the upstairs rooms, except for the one used as the family shrine. After making many inquiries of my family, I discovered that some of my sister's girlfriends had visited us. One of them had been in our family shrine for a short while. She was the only daughter of one of my father's friends. She had to be the one who did this. She was famous for being the most beautiful girl in our town. She was also well educated and a lover of literature.

Though I had never paid attention to her before, I decided I must pay her a visit. I thought of the ancient one's saying: "Three people are walking together; one of them must have something I can learn." I dressed myself neatly and directly went to see her.

She received me in the small hall of their garden. After our greeting, I politely and straightforwardly requested an explanation of the addition I was certain she had made on my study wall. She blushed and suggested that if I would call on her for ten days she would then give me her explanation. I agreed to this as my respectful lesson. Thus, every afternoon I went to her house. We read some good, ancient poetry, played Chinese chess, and did some gardening. Our friendship developed more with each day. When she tenderly touched the back of my hand, I felt that something had struck me, yet I liked it. Her eyes were the most beautiful poem I had ever read. The sweetness of her delicate smell intoxicated me. Her smile engulfed me.

Before long, however, a difficulty surfaced in our budding romance. It appeared that she was especially attached to a novel entitled *The Red Chamber*. I could never agree with her belief that *The Red Chamber* held the truth of life and, likewise, she could never agree with my Kung Fu practice.

When we reached the end of our ten-day period together, I again requested her explanation of the lines she had written on my wall. She asked for my palm, upon which she wrote a Chinese character with her gentle, slim finger. The Chinese word struck me in the same way I was struck by her finger moving lightly over my palm. It was the character for the word "love" or, more appropriately in this case, "affection."

Now I was even more bewildered than before. I could not refrain from asking her what connection could possibly exist between the love of which she spoke and her addition to my writing. At first she hesitated. Then finally, with apparent difficulty, she said, "You like to think much of Confucianism, Buddhism, and Taoism, but without the word 'love' nothing has any meaning in life. Have you ever thought of that?"

This was a real question for me. Since I had never experienced love, I had never truly pondered this question. I answered frankly, "I do not know yet. How do you know?"

"From *The Red Chamber*," she answered.

I frowned. I had read the book and did not like it. When I told her that, she responded, "What is wrong with a girl and a boy falling in love as described in that book?"

"I don't know. It seems like too much trouble to become involved in such complicated love," I replied.

"Well, it seems to me like Confucianism, Buddhism, and Taoism give you even more trouble with all kinds of study and discipline," she argued.

"I haven't thought about that. However, you have given me your explanation. I shall now go home to discover, through my own cultivation, the true significance of that word."

Though it was time to say goodbye, her eyes kept staring into mine and I felt their warmth flow into my body. Gradually, her eyes became moistened, tears falling from them like a string of pearls. I did not know how to help her.

After a long while with her handkerchief to her face, she said. "You are always contemptuous toward me and the other girls. You will not come to see me again."

"I don't know. I'll think about it," I replied.

"It will be too late to see me if you only think about it. I shall die only for love, like Blue Jade [the main female character in *The Red Chamber*]. Can you understand?" she asked.

"I shall go home and study this book that you like so much."

She offered, "I would like for you to have my copy since it is the best version." She went into her inner room to get the copy of her "holy book" and gave it to me. I took the book and left.

Though we had several versions of *The Red Chamber* in our house, I had never been able to read through any one of them in its entirety. The main story described the life of Precious Jade, a young man of a noble and wealthy family. Although his youth was spent in an elegant garden with many beautiful girls as his companions, he fell in love only with Blue Jade. However, his family arranged for him to marry a girl for whom he had no love. Soon afterward, Blue Jade died from her disappointment in love. Precious Jade's family also suffered decline. Precious Jade himself discovered that his entire life was an empty dream and thus he decided to leave the dusty world to become a Buddhist monk.

Though this book was a good work of literature, the love it described was narrow. I could not recognize any high truth with which the author could illuminate human life. However, since I would have liked to keep the girl as a friend, and because I still felt difficulty with the question of love, I turned to my mother for help.

My mother told me, "An ancient sage once said, 'Even a developed one feels trouble communicating with women and children.' Problems are created when people of different levels of development come together. Therefore, spiritual development sometimes makes it more difficult to be with ordinary people. If this shortcoming of a developed person is not moderated, it can bring extreme isolation to him. This would not be a beneficial direction for anyone to go in, unless it is done so intentionally, with a positive purpose for some special cultivation.

"Love is an important matter in life. Nobody can ignore it. In general, as you already know, love can be classified into two different categories: broad love and narrow love. Broad love is humanistic, and all the ancient sages were recognized for their broad love. Confucius [551–416 B.C.E] and Mencius [372–298 B.C.E] exalted humanistic love. Mo Tzu [501–479 B.C.E] exalted universal love and made himself as a model to realize it. He led a life of absolute self-abnegation. He exerted himself to the fullest extent of his life by working for the peace of humanity. Lao Tzu valued natural impartial love as the highest level. Shakyamuni exalted compassion and equal love. In general, humanistic love is developed, peaceful, impersonal, and dispassionate. This is what human nature was born with and what human beings should continue to cultivate. Also, in general, narrow love can only be practiced between two people, like a boy and a girl, a man and a woman, a husband and wife, or among a group of people like a family, a circle of friends, a religious fellowship, a society, a nation, or a race.

"The practice of narrow love is usually passionate. Passion means emotion. Passion is what makes love narrow. Passionate love can be a good experience during one's youth, but passion needs to be well guided and controlled. Although the emotional experience of narrow love can be beautiful, it can also be harmful. Broad, humanistic or natural love, however, can be enjoyed throughout this life and all lives. Whether love is humanistic or passionate, it should always be guided by the principle of balance. If one loses balance in the name of love, then that way of loving is unhealthy.

"All people are born with passion, yet different patterns of passion give people different temperaments. One's temperament is influenced by all the stages of one's prenatal and postnatal life. Parents must take the great responsibility to smooth their own temperaments when raising children in their prenatal and postnatal stages. An individual must also take responsibility to cultivate himself and regulate his own temperament when a certain level of growth is reached, or as the saying goes, 'An adult must take responsibility for his own ugly face.'

"Now we come to the matter of adjusting one's personal temperament. One's temperament is like one's dog: one needs to put a muzzle and leash on it when taking it in public. Surely achievement comes when one has cast off one's 'dog' nature, which is molded by the environment.

"Passion is natural. It is something we are born with, but the way we express our passion is a matter of our environment. We develop that expression ourselves, thus it is controllable and reformable.

"Passion is like water. Water is always water, but in its different phases, the speed and shape of its flow vary greatly. It can be a swift current, a big flood, or a torrent. It can be slow-moving or stagnant and motionless. It can also be a rising or ebbing tide, overflowing or draining a stream, lake, ravine, river, or ocean. When water meets heat, it becomes vapor; when it meets cold, it becomes ice. Dew, rain, hail, fog, frost, ice, snow, and so forth, all come from water. The water always remains the same—it is the environment which causes its different characteristics. Passion is like that.

"Passion is only a part of the whole human mental being, however. There is still the higher sphere of the mind which needs to be cultivated and developed so that one can have good control over the passion of the lower sphere of the mind. A raft riding the torrents cannot carry many people. Danger may be lurking anywhere along the path. Though one may enjoy the excitement of riding a raft in the torrents, this is not a normal, everyday practice. If one's passion is like a torrent, then one's life is like a raft. How dangerous that is! How long can the enjoyment of such excitement last? Is it worth exhausting one's life? This seems to be a poor model of normal, healthy passion.

"Love is a beautiful passion; however, when emotional force or possessiveness is attached to what one loves, the sublime state of pure love is degraded or damaged. Surely, a spiritually developed person can still feel personal love, but it is unattached and unoccupying love. This is the fine quality of true spiritual love. The nature of spiritual love is subtle. One can unceasingly appreciate beauty without creating the troubles which accompany its ownership. Therefore, a full life of appreciation can be lived without carrying the weight of worldly burdens.

"Out of one's humanistic love comes the courage to accept responsibility for the world. This is certainly not a rigid practice. Most ancient Taoists, if not living in the high mountains married to the beauty of nature, would travel around the world like a white cloud flying across the sky. Nothing could restrict them.

"The particular practice of love in our family is to reach the level of the ancient Taoists. We follow the external patterns of secular life, but within this everyday life we fulfill the broadness of spirituality. In other words, we use the roughness of the world and the difficulties of practical life as the friction that creates our spiritual sparks. This is what people call enlightenment or inspiration. Though enlightenment and inspiration are only momentary experiences, they can mark where one has reached. Furthermore, the endurance of life, which is built from the difficulties of worldly life, is our actual realization of universal, impartial love. The refinement of one's passions and emotions becomes an important aspect in this realization.

"Some people cannot see with their partial vision that the truth is total. They think there can be no existence of individual happiness in the practice of humanistic love, but the real truth is that individual happiness exists only in the happiness of its completeness. Can one have happiness when the entire world suffers from a flood? One can only fulfill one's own life through the harmonious fulfillment of all lives. That is why, in our family, we live for ourselves as well as for the entire world, with a clear spiritual direction."

Then my mother continued, "In the narrow sense of a family, your father is our life-maker. I am the home-maker and also a life-maker. We are all makers of a common life. We fulfill our individual duty and also assist the fulfillment of each other's duty. I am eighteen years younger than your father. I respect and love him, and he has much tolerance and understanding toward me. Actually, he treats the entire world this same way, but I am the one who has the blessing to live with him. Furthermore, your father is a man of spiritual development, thus our love is mainly spiritual rather than physical. Being spiritually linked is the source of our happiness.

"If love is true, the experience of love and deep joy occur in the same moment. It is not joyful to reminisce about a particular moment of love in the past. The enlightenment of love exists in each moment. There is no search that can find love, nor any occasion that can create love. You know love when your heart is open. The music is silent, but its harmony pervades your entire being. In that moment there is no separation.

"Love is the golden light of the sun rising within your being. It is the rose which has just opened its eyes. It is the freshness of dew or the caress of a wave on the shore—all within you.

"But the dawn becomes noon and finally evening. The

early morning dew evaporates. The rose reaches its fullness and its petals fall. A wave reaches its crest and returns to the sea. Then, does love also die? If the love within us is living, does it also die when it reaches its fullness? Can one hold that certain moment of the sun's first appearance on the horizon? Can one make love endure? At what point does the joy of love's presence become the need for its possession? When one fears it will go away or die is when the need for its possession arises. At this point love becomes contaminated with emotion and need, and its original harmony changes to dissonance. Love then reverts to the realm of duality, and the presence of Tao within our hearts is missed.

"Love can be fulfilled without becoming trapped in the web of emotional needs. We can learn from the virtue of a well which exists for all to take from. Its spring never runs dry. When our inner treasure is inexhaustible, we can provide limitless love and still remain independent and nonpossessive.

"In our tradition, we can enjoy the sunrise within us every moment. Our love is as free as the blowing wind and as enduring as a flowing river. Since we continually renew ourselves, we do not fear losing love. Our cultivation becomes our lover, for our love is Tao. Thus, love never withers, for it is continually refreshed.

"When the time comes that you feel love for someone, be gentle. Love has a delicate nature. Never be rough with it or it will be completely destroyed. Always distinguish the difference between love and desire. Love gives pleasure; desire creates pressure. Desire, loneliness, tension, and disappointment can all deteriorate the delicate nature of true love. To love is to be gentle. Tender love is truly beneficial in any circumstance. If love is not given gently, it becomes stormy. Stormy love, like stormy weather, can never last long. Generally this kind of love comes out of an imbalance in one's personality or from the pressures of an unhealthy environment.

"Young people may say tender love is weak love, but

this is not true. Motherly love is tender love. An eagle soars in the sky and finds its prey among a group of small chickens searching for food in a meadow. It quickly dives to the ground, but before it can extend its sharp claws to capture its prey, the weak old mother hen has already spread her wings and gathered all her chicks under them. She puts herself, face to face, in confrontation with the aggressor. Love can give birth to courage and courage can subdue the strong. You have witnessed this great scene many times in our country life.

"I always tell your sisters that a woman should never become emotionally competitive with her man. A man does not like to have another 'manly' person in his private life. I also tell your sisters to be responsible in family life, but not bossy. A man may have enough bosses in his life outside the family. A woman must earn love and respect from a man by being feminine and by being faithful, not by fighting or competing.

"You feel troubled about correctly responding to the love that comes from this good girl. You can love her if it is your true response. This might be the first time you sail the oceans of love. However, there is nothing to be afraid of. When the current becomes rough, keep yourself centered as usual, and get complete control of your ship. As far as I can see, this girl is not a torrential type of girl. She is more like the beautiful flow of a brooklet; the poetic feeling of her presence can calmly be absorbed.

"However, do not develop your young spiritual love into sentimental love. The love of Precious Jade and Blue Jade is not a good example of pure love. It is not healthy to imitate it. Healthy love bears the fruit of deep rejoicing; nothing can alter it and nothing can be exchanged for it. The beauty of sentimental love can earn wide appreciation on a literary level. However, if it occurs in practical life, it must be the result of an emotional imbalance or feelings of insecurity.

Above all, such imaginary love lasts for only a short time. Her imitation of Blue Jade should not be encouraged by you through helping her all day to prepare a funeral for the fallen flower petals and then helping her bury them while singing the funeral hymn. I heard she has been doing this already for years. This is a silly matter, and it is ominous to accept the suggested destiny of Blue Jade in *The Red Chamber*.

"The challenge she makes on your young spiritual authority will surely benefit you. Remember, never be bothered about those who speak or write better than you. Always be mindful of achieving your own transpiercing vision of reality. She has not developed higher than you. Her motivation could be need for love rather than spiritual communication. Now, restore your inner balance and give her an answer."

The same day, I wrote my answer to her and returned her copy of *The Red Chamber*. The following is what I wrote:

> Confucianism is my garment,
> —it is too short for me,
> Buddhism is my cane,
> —it is too weak to support me.
> Now I become a worshipper of *The Red Chamber*.
>
> I am going to help Precious Jade secularize
>   from his tedious life as a monk.
> I am going to revive his Blue Jade
>   with my Taoist Magic.
>
> [1:70–78]

Single or Married

Be happy as a paired person if you are married. If you just have a friend and stay together, then be happy with the situation. Also, be happy when you are single.

Most people when they are in a relationship would like to be single and when they are single would like to be in a relationship, which causes a lot of psychological conflict. Either way, they never feel happy, so they lose the natural fountain of their youth. They should be happy no matter what the situation is.

When related to another, maintain your independence. When you are single, keep a soft heart. Single people sometimes build up a very sharp temper by becoming used to single life. [36:93]

The Path of Married Life

Men and women who wish to be married should nurture their own energy first. The appropriate attitude and appropriate energy will enable a marriage to happen easily; you will naturally attract someone who is serious about marriage.

A spiritual person can be single or married, although marriage does affect one's concentration and demand a great deal of compromise. If you wish to be married, you must have great respect for those who follow the path of married life. It is much harder than single life; it is not simple at all.

Do not think that married people are foolish or vulgar. This is a common attitude among many spiritual people. All you can say is that the path of married life is different.

A spiritual person can be married if he or she has achieved internal unity and there are no more contradictions within his or her own being. Someone who wishes to be single and spiritual but who also desires a marriage partner will not really accept a marriage or a fixed relationship at a deep level. In the next relationship, or the next life, the person will still not be happily married unless this basic conflict has been resolved. If you wish to be married, you must form your deep inner structure accordingly and not carry on an inner battle over it.

The second thing to remember, if you wish to be paired, is to never try to force a relationship on someone else by your own will. Neither should you interfere in other people's relationships or teach or support any doctrine that disrespects the marriage relationship, interferes with the fulfillment of obligations of either party in a marriage, and thus damages the union of a family.

In order to live a spiritual life, you must learn to see and accept people as they are without differentiating between them on the basis of sex. People are people. If you expect to enter the path of married life, you must respect both sexes and not think of your own sex as either superior or inferior. If you think of men as devils or of women as foxes that are out to steal your energy, then you cannot be happily married in this or a later life. [14:231–32]

Form Does Not Affect Essence

A man might be unhappy if he thinks he is not handsome, and a woman might be unhappy about being regarded as the weaker sex. Only a spiritually achieved one is the same, whatever the form, because he or she knows that just as water takes whatever form it is in and maintains its own nature, one's form does not affect one's spiritual essence. [26:23]

Sexual Harmony

I had an interesting conversation with a friend who said he saw a movie about a man who used to habitually go drinking in bars in the evenings. The man would leave his wife at home and come back late, half drunk and sexually aroused. The woman would be in a bad mood about his arriving in a drunken stupor and would refuse him. His response was to give her a black eye. He would push her onto the bed and make her have sex with him. This type of behavior was common among the families in that particular apartment complex. The next day the women would see each other's black eyes and understand what had happened the previous night.

Another friend told me, "Those women are dumb. If I were her, I would not stay with a man like that or let him do that." This is an important issue for American women today, and that kind of behavior is partly why the women's liberation movement came into being. In this tradition, financial independence is respected, but what about women who choose to be dependent upon a reliable man and help him instead of seeking their own financial independence?

Let us go back to about five thousand years ago. When marriage was first established, a man only needed to give two pieces of deer skin or two wild geese to a woman's parents in order to marry her. Surely there were sexual demands placed on a woman in those days, too, to which she needed to respond. There are basically two ways to respond to this matter, as we shall see.

At that time, all men engaged in some type of physical work, which, unlike today's office jobs, was rather rough. The man would return from the fields or hunting, and how the evening went depended on how a woman managed the atmosphere of the home. A wise woman knew her energy and cycles. She would not make the man sexually excited, but received him gently and guided him in the living place, cooking for him, gently talking to him, and nicely guiding him to feel her gentleness and respectfulness. The roughness he gathered from his work would be dissolved by the subtle treatment of this wise woman. Wife beating did not occur in this household. Perhaps today's women should take more responsibility for the problem of disharmony.

Generally, women mature psychologically and intellectually earlier than men. Men are dumb and are easily managed, but not with fighting or competition. The approach of, "You are rough, I am also rough; you hit me, I will hit you too; you call me names, I will call you names too," does not work and only causes more disharmony. A wise woman never utilizes the same approach as a man, because their physical natures are very different. Some women have not noticed that if the man yells and she yells too, or if the man calls her names and she calls him names too, a fight will result. Well, then, who is the loser? Who is like a hen lying on the ground serving the rooster? Developed women do not behave in such a way. Before her man comes home, she has already set up a program in her mind to guide his energy. She does not guide it downward to stir up his penis, but instead guides it upward, to have a good, beautiful feeling, a sweet feeling of the gentleness of his woman. He will be satisfied that he has everything from this feeling his woman gives to him. He will not raise his fist to harm her or raise his voice to speak disrespectful words to her, because he appreciates her. He has received an education from his lady. Naturally, men cannot compete intellectually with women, but in recent times the situation has changed by women being educated the same way as men and working the same as men. Their feminine sensitivity is destroyed by the new trend. However, this is not to be stressed. . . .

Men and women do have individual differences that need to be acknowledged. In a married or related couple, each individual's talents should be recognized and used. The person without the particular talent should not have to spend excessive time and energy doing a job than the one who has the talent for it. If the man thinks that the woman is taking advantage, or vice versa, if you are constantly adding on a calculator and keeping score of what each partner does, then harmony will not occur. That is like two people staying in a hotel. That is not the way for two people to love and support each other, grow together, and enjoy life through different experiences.

Try to improve yourself. Cultivate yourself as a wise person and be ready for whatever situation may arise. Do not overly express independence from your spouse or become too self-centered. What is important in the world is that people live together. There are different types of relationships: friends, co-workers, teachers, business associates, and so on. Relationships are the texture of human life. In each moment, a man needs to exercise his understanding, brotherliness, fatherliness, patience, and tolerance in order to meet all situations with brightness and to make all situations comfortable for himself. In each moment, a woman needs to exercise her gentleness, sisterliness, motherliness, patience, and tolerance in order to make all situations comfortable for herself. [9:204–205, 213]

Attitude toward Sex

The topic of sex is something that comes up for all spiritual teachings. This is because sexual energy is the foundation of spiritual growth. Some teachers abuse it. It is best that a teaching does not have a stiff attitude toward sex, but discipline is important. Anyone engaging in spiritual learning must not have a loose attitude toward sex. If one has a suitable sexual expression, it is important to know the right way to do it, and what is beneficial and correct for oneself and one's partner. This is the correct sexual attitude at the stage of an achieved spiritual person. [25:137]

Guidelines for Health

The traditional spiritual teachings include simple and general guidelines for health which were collected by an anonymous author who lived before the Ming dynasty, using the pen name "The Hermit of the Western Mountain." These writings deal with the protection and cultivation of a human's energy. If a person does not value life and is unwilling to cultivate the energy he or she embodies, it will be impossible to transcend the painful problems and suffering created by the mind. It is futile to search for many kinds of medicine in hopes of prolonging one's physical life to an extraordinary age. Yet regulating the habits of one's ordinary daily life—such as exercise, the quality of one's thoughts and desires, the expression of emotions, the intake of food and drink—can yield tremendous rewards. If one can become free of excessiveness, one can find peace and happiness.

The basic advice concerning diet is to eat and drink with discrimination and when it is appropriate: that is, only when one is really hungry or thirsty. It is best to eat small amounts several times a day. Overeating will damage one's energy and health. Certain foods are unwholesome and to be avoided altogether. These are: cold, sticky, or hard foods; meat from sick animals or those who died a natural death; and any foods which are difficult to digest. Too many grain products will obstruct the energy flow in the body. Excessive amounts of any one of the five different flavors—salty, sweet, sour, bitter, and hot (pungent)—will damage the energy of the five viscera. Excessive salt intake, for example, causes kidney disorders. Excessive sugar consumption leads to high blood pressure and other diseases related to the condition or circulation of the blood, such as inflamed gums or headaches from blood congested in the head. Raw fish and meat may upset the digestive system, as may spicy or greasy foods. Foods which have been preserved for a long time, such as pickled foods, are to be avoided completely by the elderly and eaten only in small quantities by the young. Baked or roasted foods need to cool off somewhat because the heat will damage the gums and teeth.

In general, it is good to abstain from consuming anything which is very hot or very cold. Cold drinks in hot weather may induce a disorder of the stomach energy and may possibly cause diarrhea. If you drink wine, choose good-quality wine and drink it at room temperature and in moderation. Getting drunk damages the mind and brain, and the thirst arising out of alcohol consumption leads to a high intake of other liquids and the retention of fluids in the body. In the summer, alcohol should be avoided completely. Drinking strong tea overstimulates the brain and causes the body to become cold and less energetic. One or two cups of tea after meals, however, are permissible because they aid in digestion and dissolve the grease from foods. When one is hungry, strong tea is detrimental, but when one has overindulged in alcohol it assists in detoxification.

If dinner is eaten late in the evening, the unutilized food will produce an energy stagnation in the stomach. Retiring when one is drunk is equally harmful. On the other hand, listening to peaceful and graceful music or taking a short walk will aid the digestion. One may also massage the stomach lightly with both palms and thereafter the kidney area. Then raise the hands above the head and exhale three to five times through the mouth in order to eliminate the heat and toxins from the food. This practice is called "generating water and earth."

Practical teachings recommend some techniques and habits which are beneficial for one's energy. It is important to keep the body warm and to use warm water for bathing and brushing one's teeth. A cold bed or pillow can disturb one's energy. Combing one's hair frequently, rubbing one's face, biting one's teeth, and swallowing one's saliva help to refine one's energy. The strengthening of one's internal organs and brightening of the face is accomplished by rubbing the backs of the thumbs together to produce heat; then gently stroking over the eyes fourteen times, over the sides of the nose thirty-six times, then with the palms fourteen times over the ears and fourteen times over the face. The best sleeping position for conserving one's energy is on the side and with the knees pulled up slightly. This is a protection from the intrusion of external energies which may cause nightmares. To sleep peacefully, turn off all lights and remain silent while lying down. When awakening, it is good to stretch thoroughly.

The different seasons of the year require certain precautions. The summer especially is a difficult season for taking good care of oneself. Sweating may cause no trouble in the summer, but avoid it as much as possible in the winter, because it creates a loss of energy in the body and weakens it. In autumn and winter, stay indoors until sunrise if possible. In spring and summer, it is time to rise when the rooster crows. In the cold winter, do not rise earlier than sunrise or the rooster's crow. (A rooster usually crows during a three-hour range before sunrise.) Also, do not rise later than sunrise. Another general precaution is not to walk in the mist, in the dark, or during thunderstorms.

The body needs to be protected from strong wind, particularly when sitting or lying down and after exercise or the consumption of alcohol, both of which open the pores and increase one's vulnerability to the wind. If a constant draft on the head goes unnoticed, for example, it may cause severe headaches.

The containment of one's physical and mental desires is of great importance. Physical and mental energies need to be balanced and in harmonious interplay with each other. To be idle physically and yet entertaining a busy mind is a waste of one's energy; working diligently and keeping one's mind at leisure is a healthy way of life. If one has strong mental energy and low vitality, be careful to engage only moderately in sexual activity.

Even in such matters as looking at objects, listening to sounds, and walking or sitting, excessiveness will be a reason for disorder. The body needs exercise to remain healthy and to be full of energy, but it can suffer from unreasonable physical demands. As a general but valuable guideline, adhere to the principle of moderation in all things. Approaching each situation with moderation will assure a balanced and harmonious life. [38:64–67]

Nourishment

Do you know what kind of food is the most nourishing? The best nourishment comes from your relaxed, calm mind. If you eat good food but have a troubled mind, the results will not be good.

I remember traveling once near the boundary of China where there were many different races of people. In one place the girls were very attractive, and one of my companions became interested in someone. Eventually the parents said that he must marry their daughter and that he could not leave! So every day she gave him all kinds of food that he desired, and good wine and music, and so on, but every day he became thinner and less energetic. They finally asked him if he wanted to go, because he seemed useless. When we were back on the road, and even though we would eat very poorly at times (sometimes eating leaves off the trees), he became fat again and looked very fresh. This was just because his mind was now at ease. So before you look outside yourself for nourishment, look within and relax your nervous system and make your mind calm. A Chinese proverb says, "If a man has a happy mind, he will have a healthy body." Your inside and outside follow the same principle. In ancient China we did not know the science of nutrition and people were often undernourished, but they enjoyed longevity because they were happy. Today we have much good food and knowledge, but I do not think we are as happy or as healthy.

A Chinese proverb says, "Any man, even a beggar, during his meal is the same as the Emperor." What does this mean? When you are eating, nobody should disturb you. In China, family life was very strict, and the only time you could escape discipline was when you were eating. When I was a boy, I spent a great deal of time eating! If you are nervous and trying to eat, how can your digestive system work well? The way most of you eat is terrible; sometimes in the car, sometimes quickly and then back to work. Maybe you aren't as bad as most people, but remember that you must enjoy yourself and your food when you are eating.

The second principle I would like to mention is that we also depend on good air as much as food for nourishment. Do you know that in some very high villages in Asia they do not know about nutritional science or anything like that, but the people still live very long lives? The reason is that the air is fresh and clean. If you are forced to be in a place where the air is dirty, you must learn how to breathe correctly and take time on your days off to find a place with clean air so you can cleanse your lungs and windpipe. The principle of breathing is very simple: just breathe deeply. We have three places in the body with empty space: the head, the chest, and the belly. These three cavities must be filled with good, fresh air. Taoists depend on correct breathing very much.

The third source of nourishment is water. China is a very big country, and some parts have very good water. The people from these areas are very beautiful. If you have problems with your skin, you are probably drinking bad water. You might think that everywhere on earth the water is the same, but in some places the water can help your health and in some it is harmful. How do you decide? You decide by your developed intuition. [7:183–85]

Sleeping and Waking

Going to sleep and getting up is a specific art. To a mental worker, it is an important subject. To most physical workers, this question would be a joke—what art to falling asleep? When they go to bed, they sleep like logs; they probably could not wake up if they needed to. But if you want to learn the art of a conscious life, you do not live in a mechanical way, but live a whole life. If you want to get up early with a fresh spirit, you need to sleep well. If you wish to sleep well, then in the late afternoon and evening, you already begin to put yourself in a quiet condition, subtly, gently nurturing your energy. Going to sleep and getting up are a T'ai Chi; they cannot be separated from each other.

The late afternoon or evening is not a time to see new people, visit new places, or go to operas—I am sorry to say that to the people in the opera business. If at night you are excited by seeing an interesting show, your staying up late and getting up late will disorder the desirable normalcy of your life. In the long run, it is not beneficial for your health. However, we are talking here about the natural normalcy, not about the "normalcy" influenced by the later culture of human society. In natural normalcy, in the late afternoon or evening, you would best remain inactive. Do not be overactive and do not excite your mind. Spiritual energy, or psychic energy, is associated with the mind. Once your mind calms down and becomes quiet, you give your physical strength and nervous system a needed break.

To natural people, sleep is a refreshment, a time of fixing and restoration for the next day's functioning, and it is vitally important. Those who look deeply at spiritual cultivation view the day, including the afternoon, as a time to labor or work on many things, and the night as a time for rest and restoration. It is a cultivation, it is a cyclic pattern of regeneration. Without a good night's sleep, the next morning as you continue to follow the routine of life, you have not restored your life being to a balanced condition. It means your bank account is getting low, and if you continue to do that, you will create overdrafts. Then you will have bad credit, and even bankruptcy can occur—that means you are sick and dying. So sleep is a natural help, it is the natural system. It is Tao. Tao is nature. The natural cyclic movement gives all life time to rest.

Some people need to make their eyes feel tired, otherwise they cannot fall asleep, so they sit and watch television or read a book. Some people just sit in front of the television set for several hours to enjoy the shows or the movies. However, that is not the spiritual way. If the TV story or the book is bad and if you are a sensitive person, you pick up all the bad energy, which goes into your mental system as unhealthy, unbeneficial fodder. You may have eaten a bad dinner, you enjoy the poison dinner (some food is poison, you may not have noticed that), but it is all absorbed in your nervous system. If you feed yourself bad stuff, it will affect you most at night, because at that time you are relaxed and receptive. To one doing spiritual cultivation, it is important that the evening be serene because impressions from what you absorb will affect your dreams.

All of this is why I say that going to sleep is an art. You have to be selective with what you feed your body and mind. Peaceful, good music is appropriate. Music that is too loud or disturbing is not fitting because it stimulates you too much. Gentle walking or comfortable chatting with pleasant company is also nutritious or beneficial. If the company is not comfortable for you, even if it is a close friend, your life companion, spouse, or children, it might be best in the evening to go into your room or someplace where you can be quiet. If chatting with uncomfortable company is your daily routine, you will retain uneasiness and unpleasantness. As you go to sleep, you will carry that with you. It means the possibility of introducing an unhealthy element into your nervous system, your heart and your mind. If you are wise, you will find a gentle way to withdraw from this and go to your room and rest. However, even if you do chat with pleasant company about things not disturbing to you, it is still beneficial to be quiet awhile before you go to bed and to withdraw from everyone to quiet yourself down from the busyness and the responsibility of the day.

Gentle music and quiet activity prepare you before you go to bed. You need to nurture and brew the gentle feeling of sleepiness before you go to sleep. This is a cultivation for sleep. First put your mind already in sleep, then you will sleep well. If you lie down right away, your mind will not sleep; nor will the sleep come soon. If you already feel sleepy and you have the signal of body sleepiness, but you get to talking about something, the feeling of sleepiness will then blow away, like leaves in the wind. It is best if talking is avoided.

I cannot discuss this subject without mentioning the food you eat several hours before your rest: your dinner. Some food can cause you much difficulty in falling asleep. We are not necessarily talking about stimulating, spicy food; even food that is too hot or too cold will make your body work harder. In order not to overtax your body, the nutritious food you have prepared should not be too cold or too hot. With regard to taste, it is better not to have it too spicy or too salty. Before you go to sleep at night, it is not advisable to drink strong tea or coffee. Even citrus fruit or any fruit juice that contains strong acid can cause an astringent reaction on your nervous system, a kind of tightness that will make it hard for you to go to sleep. However, eating patterns are usually a person's strongest habits. To be a Taoist, to be a student of natural life, one of the first things you learn is to liberate yourself from being a slave of unhealthy worldly habits.

So in the evening, quietly withdraw to your room. There are a number of invocations in my *Workbook for Spiritual Development* that you can practice. Some are absolutely not fit for nighttime practice. But others are helpful because they are very gentle. You can recite them to replace the thoughts, confusion, and disorder produced in your mind by the day's activities. A mind is not easily purified. In your daily contact, work, and stimulation, contamination keeps occurring and cannot be eliminated unless you do something about it. Otherwise, it is as though you were playing an old tape or an old record over and over again. So in the evening time it is beneficial to recite the instruction for masters, the customary spiritual instruction. That is beneficial; even if you lie down, you can still do it. Then gently fall asleep with those good instructions.

Form a good habit; before you go to bed, urinate and empty your bowels so that you can sleep more comfortably and without interruption . . .

So you have had enough sleep. Now you might ask me again, since you are a human being, when do you have sex? If you are truly serious about your spiritual cultivation, my recommendation is to avoid sex if you find that you are not strongly desiring it. If you have sex, surely it is preferable to do it in the early evening, at a time when it will not affect your normal sleep. There is a lot of knowledge about doing sex; for example, doing sex for fun, as a medicine, for energy adjustment, or to have children. If some people do not have sex, they become crazy; so they need to find a healthy way to do it. However, remember that when you have sex, there should not be any disturbance in your mind. A peaceful night with moonlight or starlight, not a night with a storm or strong wind, is best. Do it in a correct location, not too close to a cemetery or someplace like that. If your purpose is to have children, it is especially important to watch those elements; otherwise you can never have a healthy baby with a bright future. Never use aids or stimulants. You may do well at sex or not. Mostly it is another art, but for the purpose of spiritual cultivation, it is not suitable to take your focus away from sleeping.

Now we come to the next morning. Morning time is so important. If you need to get up and you cannot, immediately put your hand to the back of your head and scratch it; scratch it, and do not stop until the energy fully rushes to your head. Do not stop until you get up and dress. Waking up is also an art.

I have mentioned that when you go to sleep, let your mind be the first part of you to fall asleep. Conversely, when you wake up, let your mind be the first to wake up. If your body is still in sleep, you need to scratch the back of your head, or any part of your head, to wake up the whole body. Once the energy is rising to your head, the whole body will easily and peacefully come back to the correct awakened order. When your life is light, your sleep is light and your waking up is also light. Otherwise it is all hard and you struggle. The moment when you wake up is so important. If you do not awaken, what do you do? You fall into the dream state. Dreams take away more of your energy than your daily work. In Taoist cultivation, dreams are energy which can be controlled to support your work on immortality and spiritual achievement.

Therefore, it is better to wake up early, before five o'clock. If your mind wakes up and your body is still asleep, many different dreams may occur. In some dreams you see a vision of what will happen later that day. Because the human brain is so powerful, it can foresee things that will take place and know what you are going to do. But even those dreams are not beneficial. What is better is just to get up before any dreams begin. [16:116–23]

Bedtime

Do not read a book just before you go to bed. If you read a book under light, your eyes will become congested with blood. If you are very interested in the subject of that book, you will concentrate more on it and the blood will gather in your brain, and when you go to bed you will have trouble falling asleep or sleeping well. People who have trouble falling asleep may sometimes need to watch something to make their eyes tired so that they can go to sleep, but this is not good energy management.

For people who do a lot of mental work during the day, I do not suggest very vigorous exercise or going to the gym in the evenings. Their nervous system will become tight from the exercise and it will be hard to relax. In the evening it is most helpful to do a little bit of gentle movement, such as taking a walk in a safe, quiet place. Those who work mentally have a heavy load in daytime and find it hard to stop thinking in the evening. Thinking gathers the blood in the brain, so walk in a quiet place, not thinking too much, and the blood will more evenly distribute to the limbs and trunk of the body. Or before you go to sleep, soak your feet in warm water. Washing your feet before you go to bed is a good habit and will help you sleep peacefully. But do not take a shower or bath in the late afternoon or evening time. Especially, do not wash your head. If you wash your head at this time, it will be full of energy and your rest will not be sound enough at nighttime.

People who do physical work usually become very tired by the work and sleep like a log. They do not need knowledge of how to fall asleep, if they are not overexhausted from the day. [9:221]

Self-Inspection

Putting on a robe and sitting down will not make you a saint. Pasting on a wispy beard will not make you a wise one. What you must do is give yourself some self-education. In order to educate yourself you should practice self-inspection frequently, especially at night. Do not continually run out to movies or parties in order to rely on someone or something external to calm you down or pacify you. Instead of attempting to escape from yourself, try to help yourself. Do not be afraid to just sit quietly and do the self-adjustment that only you can do. It is all really up to you. You might even be surprised to discover some new and interesting things about yourself. The truth is that everything is already there; you only need to discover it. Self-discovery is a very important thing, no less important than Columbus's discovery of the New World. So some night when you come home from work, try to eliminate all outside influences, sit quietly, and see yourself clearly. Do not rush to turn on the TV or radio or pick up the newspaper. Instead, do something helpful for yourself. Do not waste your precious time trying to satisfy every impulse you have. Those impulses simply indicate that your energy has gone to that area of your body. When the energy goes to the eyes you desire to read something or watch TV; when it goes to your limbs you get restless to walk or run; and when it goes to the groin, sexual desire becomes strong. So take time to reflect about your impulses to see if they are beneficial or not.

For instance, women sometimes have the urge to become a mother. This is a serious decision and should not be the result of an impulse. If you get involved with an irresponsible man and have a baby, that baby will suffer for many years because of your error. Men are no more lucky than women when it comes to child rearing since they also have many problems to face during these years.

Please use the nighttime as your quiet time. Do not substitute TV for your own reflection and self-cultivation. Be brave and examine your errors and weaknesses. If you never correct yourself, you will live your whole life erroneously and create many problems for yourself.

So what are some of the practical things you can do on your path of self-discovery? First, be flexible and willing to change your personality and the way you think. Many foolish people say that there is nothing wrong with the way they think, but let me say that it is their incomplete knowledge of life which is the first great obstacle to true well-being.

You often check your cars to see if there are any small troubles so that nothing serious ever develops. But do you ever take time to check out your mind and emotions to see if there is some problem? Or do you wait until it is so serious that you need a major overhaul? If you would adjust yourselves a little every day, you would not have such big problems. So the first suggestion is to observe and adjust yourself every day. Only you can make the effort. As the saying goes, "A one-thousand-mile journey begins with the land under your feet." In other words, the highest spiritual achievement comes from your daily life and how well you pay attention to every detail.

So, every evening, while keeping your mind and emotions calm, take a journey into yourself and learn something about yourself that can benefit your entire life. A good practice is to use a diary or tape recorder, but remember that words can be great imposters. Do not let your mind trick you.

Fight for your spiritual life. Do these practical things and you will gain a deeper understanding of yourself and will not be enslaved by the need of the physical and lower biological spheres, namely the genital glands and reproductive organs. [8:160–61]

Dreaming

Some people are able to cause a response of the subtle energy through their dreams, and others are not: some dreams cause response, while others do not. The response may be on the physical or on the spiritual level. Dreams are more subtle and therefore more difficult to control than daytime behavior.

There are two categories of dreams. One type of dream is caused by messages from within the body. As one's energy circulates through the body, it passes by and stimulates the nerves of different parts of the body which will transmit messages to the brain. In other words, the energy tells stories about the real feelings and images of body and mind in the form of a mental stage play. The different spheres and parts of the body through which the energy flows will cause the brain to be stimulated in various areas, creating distinct impressions in one's consciousness.

The other type of dream is caused by messages received from outside the body. These dreams may be rehearsal of an event that will happen in the future, the telepathic message that something is happening thousands of miles away, or a communication from another being. This type of dream happens when one's own subtle energy connects with the subtle energy of an event or another being.

Usually, highly evolved people have no dreams because they have few desires. The peaceful mind sleeps lightly. The reality of your life is the reality of your mind. The most useful and valid dreams occur when your energy is connected clearly, straightly, and directly with your internal or external energies. Then the message to your consciousness will also be straight and clear. By cultivating your energy well, you will be able to guide your dreams and use them advantageously.

Master Lieh Tzu said:

> *A dream is an energy that comes into contact with the mind; an external event is an energy that impinges on the body. Hence our feelings by day and our dreams by night are the result of contacts made by body and mind. It follows that if one can concentrate one's mind in abstraction, one's feelings and dreams will vanish by themselves. Those who rely on their waking perceptions will argue about them. Those who put faith in dreams do not understand the processes of change in the internal and external energy cycles. "The pure men of old passed their waking existence in self-oblivion and slept without dreams." How can this be dismissed as an empty phrase?*

The following invocation may be used to cleanse the unpleasant or frightening shadow remaining from the experience of a bad dream and to prevent its occurrence in the physical reality of life; it must be practiced diligently and properly. It is called the "Purification from Heaven and Earth."

Heaven and Earth are spontaneous manifestations
    of the wondrous, universal law.
As the original oneness expresses itself,
    gross and subtle energy become distinctly divided.

My "Bodily Cave" is brightly illuminated
    by the mysterious light from the three sources,
    my three tan-t'ien.

The powerful spirits of the eight directions
    conjoin my being with the true origin of life.
By the absolute order of the divine Ling Pao*
    in the highest Ninth Heaven,
      send the positive energy of Chien Luo, Tan Na,
      Dan Kan, and Tai Shuan† to destroy my spiritual
      obstacles and debilitate any evil influences.
For this divine invocation
    is given to the highest sovereignty.
It is a jade oracle from the Subtle Origin.
I read this invocation with strong sincerity
    to drive away the demons and evils
    in order to lengthen my years.
With this order, the attained spirits respond to me.
The evil demon king, Mu Wang, is chained to stand as
      my guard and servant.
The negative atmosphere has been cleansed.
The Ch'i of Tao is everlasting.
So it is commanded.
[38:133–35]

---

*The heavenly reverent spiritual authority.
†These are the most powerful energies in nature and are named as spiritual guardians.

Seasonal Changes

The period at the change of the four seasons is when people can have physical trouble like the flu. If you use medication or other unnatural methods to treat it, then other internal troubles will manifest in different ways.

If you know the natural annual cycle, you know beforehand how to adjust to the seasonal changes. This is important for learning how to live longer and healthier and it is one elucidation of learning the Way.

In the hot season, you can eat less, you can fast, you can have sex a little more frequently if your diet is light and you are active outdoors.

In the cold season, eat more nutritiously, do not do a serious fast, decrease or stop sexual activity. Your diet can be rich, but do not stay outdoors too long.

In spring and summer, your head should be to the east when you sleep. In autumn and winter, your head should be to the west when you sleep. Head to the north should be avoided; it causes a disorder of the brain's electricity. [26:38–39]

Drive Away the Clouds

When your three internal entities are not unified, your heart is sad, your mind is full of ideas, and your soul is depressed. This is a poor way to live. A good healthy life comes from the union of your mind, your heart, and your soul in one piece. This is like the sun and the moon and the stars in an orderly sky when everything is shining and there are no clouds or storms, no rain or snow, just a beautiful sky. People whose lives are full of rain and storms never experience the wholeness of these three as one.

The first practice is never to pull any external thing into your internal being to obstruct the wholeness of your internal energy. When the three inner beings are together, we call it concentrated or converged energy. A rigid practice would block such convergence. It must be accomplished through gentle, methodical practice.

The second is that when you discover you are thinking in your meditation, immediately unite the initial energy of the thought with the awakening energy of stopping the thought: join the head and the tail of your consciousness to become one. If you get stuck anywhere, your meditation and your peaceful mind can be destroyed or disturbed by your thoughts, and the effects of your meditation can be nullified. You must realize that thoughts are energy movement. When you discover that you are thinking, immediately combine that awakening energy with the thought energy: let the two points come together without being separate, like a snake gradually swallowing its own tail.

A thought can be a solidified energy form. When you break through its form, tremendous energy and power are released. Such power is illustrated when an atom is split; the tightly bonded, interacting energy pattern of yin and yang is then integrated back into the oneness of the all-powerful subtle origin.

The third thing is that on a moonlit night, when there are clouds, would you drive away the clouds or the moon? It is important to think of your mind as the moon. Take away your cloudy thoughts, but keep the bright and shining moon.

The fourth thing is to maintain centeredness. When

emotion and insufficient knowledge are underlying your thoughts, extremes will be expressed in two ways: one is to go to the left and the other is to go to the right. You should stay centered in the midpoint, remaining neutral and above the pull of either side. When a thought arises in your meditation, do not follow or join it, and do not try to counteract it with emptiness. Do not do anything. Let what is be the way it is. This will store and dam up the subtle Ch'i. In this way you will eventually attain clarity and objectivity, which will enable you to reach the deepest essence of the mind.

These principles are applicable to your general daily life as well as your spiritual cultivation. First, the union of the three: your heart and mind and soul should always be together without any separation. Second, always be alert when you fall into thought and your peaceful mind is disturbed. As soon as you wake up from the flow of thoughts, use that point of awakening to unite with the beginning point of the thoughts. When a point starts moving, it produces time and space. If it stops moving, then it does not produce experience or time in the common sense. It is not necessary to have the feeling of concrete gravity, but it is important to make the beginning of two thoughts immediately hit each other to stop further wasteful thinking. Third is to remove the clouds without removing the bright moon. Fourth is to cut away all extremes and remain in the center. In this way, your spiritual energy will become stronger and stronger. The purpose of stronger spiritual energy is to save you from mistakes and from causing trouble for yourself and for other people. If everyone achieved this, there would be no more wasteful trouble in the world.

Most human problems are the result of conceptual conflicts among mentally and spiritually undeveloped people. Even though they think they are very intelligent and wise and developed, they are not at all. In reality, they are just like teenagers who think they know everything. They have the ability to make trouble, but their minds and their spirits are not developed enough to not make trouble. [14:210–11]

Breathing Exercise

One typical instruction from those who attained spiritual development is to get rid of what is worn out or old, and to receive what is new and fresh. This principle should be applied to your body and mind.

Breathing is an example of this principle. Every minute we exhale used air and then inhale fresh new air. This allows us to continue living a good life.

Breathing exercises can be done in many ways. Here is the main instruction:

In the clear morning, face east and stand close to a good, healthy tree to do breathing exercises. Breathe through your nose, unless stated otherwise.

1. Open your mouth to "poof" or blow out the used air. Gently, deeply inhale the fresh air, then "poof" (exhale) the used air. Repeat two more times. If you have bad breath, breathe deeply until it changes. This is the basic practice.

2. In order to enhance your body, inhale five times for each exhale. You may do this for up to ten or fifteen minutes.

3. If you are internally weak, you need to learn to hold the breath and a simple posture or movement adopted from Dao-in or simply hold the breath as

long as possible. This can be repeated for up to twenty or thirty minutes. This will invigorate your internal system by creating a benign pressure.

If you get dizzy by breathing strongly for so long, adjust the length of time you hold the breath and the length of time you spend doing the exercise. You can do this practice lying down for safety.

4. Inhale deeply, pushing the diaphragm down to fill the lower trunk. Use this method of breathing to increase your vitality.

5. When you inhale, fill the whole trunk with air. Exhale soundlessly.

6. I recommend that you learn and use only one style of breathing over a period of time. If you do exercise number 4 or 5, your abdomen will enlarge, so you should try to control the muscle of the lower tant'ien (lower abdomen) during inhales. I understand that for both men and women, a stretched or enlarged abdomen does not look attractive.

7. The instruction for breathing while you are sitting in meditation is to breathe gently, soundlessly, and evenly. For those with thin bodies, the inhale should be longer than the exhale. For those whose bodies are heavy, make the exhale a little longer than the inhale. If you try to rush the effect in order to lose weight by overly lengthening the exhale, and if you practice this for a very long time, you are doing it too much and you will become strengthless and weak. This has no benefit.

Doing good breathing exercises can improve your health and your emotional life. In order to achieve better results and reduce any trouble, you may need help from an instructor or from people of experience and achievement. [26:28–31]

Five Energies Meditation

Every day you should spend from twenty minutes to two hours harmonizing and adjusting your internal energy. If you can balance your emotions, you will have no anger or sadness and will not be easily excited. In doing this Five Energies meditation, it does not matter what position you sit in, but it is important that you are not disturbed during the time that you do it. So unplug your telephone.

As you sit, you correspond a specific color to certain internal organs. Begin with the heart and visualize red Ch'i or a soft red cloud that is transformed from your heart and watch it carefully with your internal vision. After a few minutes, watch the red cloud move to the area of the stomach and then gradually change to become yellow. This is a pure mental practice; you need to do it until there is no "me," only clouds. From the stomach, the cloud moves up to the region of the lungs, expands to cover both lungs, and becomes white. Then, after a while, the white cloud sinks down to the kidneys and bladder where it becomes dark, like the water of the North Sea, deep, dark blue with a little gray in it. This cloud surrounds all your water organs and then moves up to the liver area just to the right of your spleen and gallbladder. When it comes to this region, it changes from blue-black to green. From here, you can begin the cycle over again by moving the green cloud to the heart where it becomes red, and so forth.

Do this cultivation calmly and gently, following the

order I have given you. Do not change the order. Water gives birth to wood energy, which gives birth to fire; fire gives birth to earth, and earth gives birth to metal; metal gives birth to water and the cycle repeats itself. By your visualization, you burn away negative energy, and your internal movements harmonize your sexual energy beautifully. People are made of living energy. Someday the physical house of your soul will die, but these five clouds will be your new home that can carry you flying. The minimum goal of this practice is to fortify your energy and balance yourself.

Be gentle when you do it; be gentle when you stop it. After several circulations, you should take a break or stop. If you have done the circulation for two hours, then slow down before you bring it to a close. Collect your energy back to its original order. Just calm down. You do not need to use strength to do it. Use your gentle mind.

The second stage of the Five Cloud Meditation is to sit quietly and visualize the center of the chest or the area one half inch above the navel. I recommend that women use the point in the center of the chest. [14:159–60]

Basic Spiritual Self-Protection

- Do not worship spirits below your own spiritual development, nor an idol whose image is bewildering.

- Do not accept gifts from people who have bad or low energy.

- Do not be receptive to people or things with low or bad energy; receptivity to such energy might damage your spiritual health.

- Do not read books written by authors whose energy is confused or gross. Songs, music, and art which may have been created with a distorted vision should also be avoided or they may lead to ill effects.

- Do not accept methods or advice from people with a low character or inferior virtue.

- Do not visit or stay in places where the energy is unhealthy. Do not live in a house or place that has bad energy.

- Do not ingest food or drink if it is bad. Do not eat fruit from an unhealthy tree. Do not drink water from a bad well. Do not take meat from an animal who died of disease or other unnatural causes.

- Do not adopt rigid diets. A correct diet should allow for differences of age, work, sex, stages of cultivation, or other special considerations such as illness or pregnancy.

- Do not undertake activities with people whose energy is low or bad, especially eating, sitting, living, traveling, or partnering activities.

- Do not visit the sick or attend funerals unless it is absolutely unavoidable; special purification is needed after such visits.

- Do not allow personal items such as clothes or books to be used by other people, in order to avoid an energy mixup. Also, for this reason, your bed or personal room should not be disturbed by others.

- Do not look at either a corpse or bloodshed. If either is seen, then a special purification should be performed as soon as possible.

- Do not celebrate birthdays. They only aggrandize the ego and negatively strengthen personal bad karma. Age should not be a matter of either pride or resentment. Being young and being old are both unreturnable stages.

- Do not take long baths; however, clean yourself often.

- Do not speak of sickness or death during meals, and try to avoid these topics as much as possible at other times.

- Do not quarrel, argue, or fight in your home environment, in order to prevent violating the peaceful energy of your house. Avoid such behavior as much as possible to avoid having your normal energy flow violated.

- Do not engage in physical contact, such as shaking hands, hugging, or friendly kissing, with persons of poor or confused energy. Such people are also to be avoided when it comes to healing in any form, such as massages. Haircuts, manicures, and other similar things should be avoided. The more you do for yourself, the better.

- Do not become close to psychologically imbalanced, emotionally troubled, or overly aggressive people, regardless of how attractive they may appear. Engaging in their company may lead to disturbance or poisoning of your energy.

- Always remember that there is no reason to keep away from those people whose positions are inferior, whose finances are poor, and whose opportunities are few. But there are reasons to stay away from those whose energy is confused, low, bad, or rough.

- Do not show off your name, house, or companions, in order not to fall into worldly traps.

- Do not overly expand in any aspect of your life. Do not lose the flexibility to correct any trouble and collect yourself in due time.

- Do not divulge, in ordinary conversation, your personal spiritual discipline and practice. There also should be no disclosure whatsoever of your subtle virtuous practice. If your virtue is discovered by others, you should not take credit for it.

- Do not extend curiosity to what other people leave on the road or to what people do behind closed doors, or to what kinds of spiritual worship others engage in. Do not go into temples or other spiritual places to which you yourself are not spiritually connected; such visits may cause sickness or death.

- Do not take interest in the craft of a sorcerer. All ancient traditions are involved with some sorcerers, and though their power is invisible, it is absolutely not high divine power. The great ancient teachers have kindly pointed out that such an ability is not the important practice on the path of eternal life, nor is it the way to obtain eternal life. On the contrary, such powers usually create more spiritual obstacles for those who indulge in spiritual power practices. In most cases, the price is too high. This kind of practice is actually a type of darkness developed before people attained high enlightenment as revealed in the *Tao Teh Ching*.

- If your virtue is not sufficient to attain high spiritual achievement, your ambitions of obtaining spiritual power will suffer bitter trials. In reality, it is not necessary to strive for spiritual power or "fancy" enlightenment. So-called enlightenment may only serve to detoxify the poison of the mind. The real cultivation of immortal transcendental life is simple and easy. You only need to drive away the darkness and ready your virtue.

- Do not emphasize any spiritual power or gift that you have developed. Instead, maintain constant health and balance in all aspects of life as a sound foundation for real spiritual development.

- Maintain a basic note and low profile in your life. Cultivate honest and earnest natural ways of growth rather than looking for unusualness, strangeness, or extraordinariness in your spiritual practices. These are merely seductive qualities that typify the spiritual immaturity of some colorful and fancy religions.

- Ignore the praise given to you by ordinary people. They do not know the truth about themselves or you. Such ignorant compliments can be poisonous enough to spoil the firmness of your willpower or enlarge your ego. Instead, value the straight words or scolding from an achieved one who knows you better than you know yourself. His words you cannot buy; they are the real medicine.

- Do not work just for the feeling of happiness; it will cost you too much. It is better to remain right and true on all occasions and at every moment. The feeling of happiness belongs to the emotional level. Thus, be careful not to become a slave to your emotions; rather, be the lord of your spirit.

- Do not enjoy idleness; learn from flowing water, which never decays. Therefore, during both day and night always be gently in motion. Let your movement come from your creative nature, like the sun, moon, and stars. Be a spontaneous expression of life without asking anything in return. Through your subtle recognition, follow the natural rhythms of life and cycles of nature harmoniously, both inside and outside, in order to make your life durable for spiritual achievement.

- Do not exhaust yourself through insatiable physical or mental desires. Do not overuse one particular organ or part of your body. Overusing the body will cause your mind to become dull, and overusing the mind will weaken the body. Both forms of excess create obstacles to your spiritual growth and damage the wholeness and balance of your being.

- Avoid continuous rough physical labor such as operating heavy or strongly vibrating machinery. This can have a bad influence on your spiritual sensitivity.

- Do not engage in low-quality mental activities. Indecent, illusory, or imaginary exaggeration in writing, talking, thinking, or reading can cause your mind to become irresponsible to the correctness of your own being. The mind may become wild and lose control, finally causing you to lose the vision of the true way. To a spiritually developed person, thinking functions as the accumulation of Ch'i. Thus, when you are thinking, avoid thinking of bad things or of people with bad energy. With your thinking you may cause something to happen or you may accumulate improper Ch'i.

- All energy protection maintenance and spiritual practice in general should be done tactfully and with discretion. One's developed instinct and intuition will provide the guidelines for the proper time, place, and manner in which these practices are best pursued.

[8:237–41]

Invocation

Learn to change your consciousness, which means the thoughts you think each moment you are awake. Learn to recite passages that inspire you from the spiritual books. You can use certain paragraphs or invocations which you think are beneficial to your particular stage of spiritual cultivation. Recite them when you have time and your mind is free. Recite them each moment you do not have a particular focus in thought or when you wish to jump out from your habitual thought-stream. If you do not know how to manage your mind, when your mind is not occupied with something in particular, it can make you feel bad. So when your mind is free, recite those rewarding, beneficial paragraphs from the spiritual books. If you are a student of Tao, they can be the ones in my books, because they can help you transfer your emotion or change the focus from a lower to a higher sphere. It is wise to constantly use a recitation in quiet meditation or in the hours when you are alone. [36:93]

Praying

Prayer is the communication of one's needs or desires to a higher power such as to God or a particular name. Through prayer one may cause the response of the subtle energy. All religions stress communication between human beings and their concept of a divine sovereign. Prayer, whether embellished or simple, is generally the vehicle through which this communication is transmitted. Despite the fact that most people use prayer primarily as an emotional release, it is beyond doubt that a sincere and consistent prayer will cause a subtle energy response. However, one must be unemotional and have a disciplined mind in order to cause an appropriate response.

Different cultures and traditions emphasize particular names of images as the objects of their prayers. In fact, people may direct their prayers to any object and they may still receive a response. In ancient China, for example, people would pray to a well, the "water" energy; the kitchen stove, the "fire" energy; to very old trees, the "wood" energy; to high mountains, the "earth" energy; or to ancient swords and weapons, the "metal" energy, and they would receive a response through their sincerity. The response is also influenced by the energy of the person who uses the objects toward which the prayer is directed. In some parts of India there are temples dedicated to rats and snakes, and prayers to these spirits have also caused responses. People who have prayed to an empty house or room have received an energy response through their own soul power, just as they have through praying to anything else.

The truth is that the responsive subtle energy is everywhere in the universe and also within the person who prays. The response will be positive if the subtle energy waves are projected properly. The responsive energy is not bound by images or names, which may become obstacles to direct communication with it. Yet, because the frequency of the projected vibration is an essential factor, the vibration created by the use of the correct name of an energy is the real secret of spiritual traditions. However, when people adopt names out of their ignorance of spiritual truth, they hinder the liberation of their souls.

The phenomenon of energy response may be explained in two ways. One would be to say that the objects are powerful enough to assist the minds of the praying people in the performance of these miracles. The other way would be to say that the corresponding phase of energy evolution responds to the cause of the prayer. The truth is that human nature and the nature of the universe are one and the same. There is no distinction between individual energy and universal energy.

The teachings of the Integral Way use specific invocations which are designed to create effective and appropriate responses. The following invocation is addressed to the "Jade Emperor," which is the directing energy of the multi-universe. It is called "Daily Communion with the Jade Emperor" and is practiced for spiritual centering.

In the vastness of the universe
    there are many heavenly realms.
In the center of each
    resides its own Jade Emperor,
    the universal Master.
While appearing as many,
    in substance all Jade Emperors are one.
The "Undecayed One" is his divine title.
His true name is "Self-So."
The universe is his body
    and cosmic law his uniting principle.
He is the mind of the known
    and the eye of the unknown.
The giving and taking of life
    are his self-expression
    and the exercise of his eternality.

People are his spiritual offspring
    and the heavenly born nobility.
Because they are self-corrupting
    they lose their pristine high qualities.
The Jade Emperor reestablishes himself in humankind
    as a still and flexible mind.
The self-commanded and easy mind
    is the government of the Jade Emperor in man.
The only command he gives to his moral descendants
    is to live in harmony with the natural cosmic
order.

He educates them with self-knowledge,
    and self-refinement is the venerable rank
    he confers to them.
He bestows his blessings
    upon those of self-cultivation.
Self-contentment is the reward
    he gives to his divine lineage.

To those of high self-awareness
    his heavenly assignment
    is the realization of their divine nature.
He fulfills the one who has self-dignity
    and establishes the one who renounces himself.
He subdues no one as he regulates the universe.
He favors those who help themselves
    and hinders those who are slothful and inert.
He gives energy to those who have positive virtue
    and takes it away from those who have self-
doubt.
Self-contradiction is the punishment
    he gives to the vulgar-minded.
He brings calamity to the overly self-concerned
    and delivers tragedy to the self-indulgent.
Shock and misfortune are his warnings
    to those who are self-deceived.
He shackles those who have self-pity
    and blinds the opinionated.
He chains the self-centered
    and penalizes excessive self-love and self-hate.
Simplicity is his great teaching
    and harmony his abiding principle.
Egolessness is his key
    for the attainment of greatness.
Selflessness is his secret
    for the achievement of immortality.
He is most supreme
    because he is self-forgetting.
The clarity and purity of his being
    is the source of all fulfillment.
He is the unruling ruler of all life.

Another invocation for general use is the "Daily Mental Discipline":

I am the offspring
    of the divine nature of the universe.
Through the extension of the positive, creative,
    and constructive nature of the universe,
      I have received life.
Let pure, positive energy display itself
    in my nature and daily life.
Let only the highest energy
    be exhibited in my speech and behavior.
In my relationships with my fellow men and women,
    let me demonstrate the benevolence
    of the universal nature.

Let pure, positive energy
    be the only experience of my being.
Let my spirit and mind be a reflection
    of the sublime order and harmony of the
universe,
    and my body an expression of the Subtle Origin.
When eating, let the pure and positive nature
    nourish me directly.
When sleeping, let the peaceful nature refresh me.
When working, let the divine nature
    be expressed through me.
Let my life follow the Way of universal nature.

Let my life be the realization
    of the divine nature of the universe.
So that I can be the positive manifestation
    of the Subtle Origin
    and unite myself firmly
    with the incorruptible spirit,
    the Jade Emperor,
    the supreme core of the universe.

[38:121–25]

Two Kinds of Walking

Every day, in the morning or evening, or both, take a walk in a safe and peaceful environment for less than an hour. This can be a great fountain of youth. Choose a place to walk that has no kind of disturbance. Walking done in a work environment and when your mind is busy is different; it is not as nutritious as the walking you do for yourself in the morning or evening in a quiet, peaceful, and safe place.

There is also another useful kind of walking. It is walking away from nervous confrontations with somebody in your office or family. Walk away so that you can walk back. If you stay there, you become unpleasant or you let other people become unpleasant, which is not wise. After you walk away, give the other person or yourself time to straighten out emotionally, then walk back. This kind of walking away is usually beneficial and useful. [36:89]

Quiet Watching

Here is a typical Taoist meditation that you can do outdoors. I do not know if there is a better term to use than the words "quiet watching." The method is the traditional outdoor meditation of quietly watching an object. It has great power and can affect your emotions, your spirits, and your personality if you practice it for the correct amount of time. I have personally experienced the benefits of being trained in the outdoor meditation of quietly watching an object. The following are some examples.

Watching the sky. Lie down in an open meadow on a fine day and look up the sky. A few floating white clouds pass across the deep blue. The deep blue indicates the depth of the sky. What you can reach is only the blue color, not the depth of inexhaustible space. As you quietly watch, do not be disturbed by any passing object, especially the flying clouds. This will guide you to reach the depth of your own mind and spirit. Do this meditation, especially if you are a rushing, hasty type of person. Use it to reach your depth.

Watching the mountain. Sit quietly some distance away so that you can have the whole mountain in view. By observing it, you can learn its independence and grandness or smallness. It does not yield; it stands there, year after year.

Watching a waterfall. Sometimes emotions can be destructive to oneself or to one's environment; nature is the cure. Go to a place with a big waterfall and sit near the bottom, but not where you will get wet. By looking at the waterfall coming down from the sky, you will be washed and cleansed by it. Your emotions and your psychological experiences will all be washed away. The water comes from the highness of the mountain; it rushes down to hit the pond or stones beneath it, pounding through the obstacle in your life. Through perseverance, a stone gives way and is shaped by water. Also, by the action of the water, a pond is formed. Use the waterfall to cleanse away your worries, the contamination from your experiences in the world, and your disappointed thoughts about something that has failed or something that cannot come back.

Watching the tide. Sit at a safe place by the side of the ocean or harbor. When the big tide comes rushing in to attack the stones at the shore, sit quietly and watch. No matter how strong the tide is, remain in quietude. On the one hand, you are the tide rushing to the shore, but on the other hand, you are the shore where the rushing water stops. From the two forces, movement and stillness, you will attain the unity that exists above the conflict.

Watching the white clouds. In a late spring, summer, or autumn afternoon, you will see the billowing white clouds in the sky transforming into cities, mountains, villages, or animals. Some clouds bring very pleasant scenes or figures, but some do not. All the things you see have no connection to you, just quietly sitting there. They are so remote from you. Allow everything to transform in front of you without attempting to manage them or to keep them the same. Similarly, objectively watch your life, all experiences, and all events. Let them pass by. Let your spirit attain calmness and quietude. You become achieved by training it to watch the transformation of beauty or ugliness, of different colors and shapes of clouds, without building attachment to them. Clouds can also carry you far, far away, but do not allow yourself to be carried away; always find yourself unmoved.

Then in your life, when you have thoughts or troubles, bad or good experiences, let them be the clouds, because you have already formed and trained yourself by watching the clouds in the sky. Let the clouds carry themselves away but your spirit be independent. Also, when you have problems in your life, go into your garden, raise your head, and look at the clouds and sky above you. Your training will return to you in a few moments, and you will find calmness and detachment from your troubles.

Watching the bonfire. In experiencing the cruelty of the world, you have been disappointed and frustrated. You have been pushed into a cold corner, and your heart has become iced over. You do not find any hope in your world. You do not find any good friend in your world. You do not find any good support in your world. So sit at a right distance to watch a fire in a fireplace or bonfire. Let the fire burn away all your troubled thoughts. Let it burn off all the cruel experiences. Warm your cold heart. Let your heart return to warmth. Although people in the world may treat you badly, imagine that they treat you as though you were the one being sacrificed in life to the unseen deities. Let your feelings be burned as the sacrifice in the fire. Let it cleanse you. The warmth will reward you, revitalize your heart, renew your interest in life, and reactivate your courage to confront any difficulty in life. It will enhance your bravery to move into your bright future.

Watching the still pond or well of pure water. The water in the pond is so crystal-clear, you can even see fish swimming in it. Sit near it quietly, letting your mind be the water. All the fish enjoy the freedom of swimming in the pond; they are not bothered by wind, because they are in the water of life, not the water of death. Why allow your mind to be so crowded with negative thoughts? Learn from the example of the pond so that no thought or emotional experience bothers you. By watching the well or pond, you attain calmness. There is no source of disturbance in your sight.

Watching the evergreen trees. In wintertime, the proud and undefeated spirit of these trees does not yield to the pressure of the cold or snow. Quietly standing year after year without winking or frowning, all the needles or leaves stretch and grow as they should, undisturbed. The straight, sturdy trunk is the root of your life. Observe it to help you regain your strength of life in adverse conditions or in the cold world.

Watching the blossoming flowers. In spring, summer, autumn, and even winter, flowers are blooming. They take their support from the weather, continuing to bloom despite inclement weather. No human individual need be withered by the negative circumstances in life. Let your life blossom like those flowers, in the sense of the fullness of your spirit and fullness of your life strength.

I have gained support from these meditations in my

personal training. A sincere practice has helped me in times of mental and emotional upset amid the pressures of an un-natural world. I have gained life force, especially the subtle life force of spirit, from this type of outdoor meditation in the natural environment. By practicing them, the victory of life will also be yours.

The Nutrition of Light and Dark

People are concerned about their finances and their nu-trition. In this section, I would like you to study the nutrition that you do not need to pay for. It is the free wealth of nature that you can take as you wish.

Daylight: The most beneficial hour in a day is at dawn, when there is a shift from darkness to light. At that moment, the light is very nutritious for your nervous system, eyesight, internal organs, and also your spirits. Many people do not know how to utilize the dawn's light. It is a special secret of this hour. Especially for spiritual cultivation, your spirit will become stronger if you use the minutes from darkness to light to sit up, do spiritual practice, walk in the garden, or do gen-tle movement.

Sunlight and Moonlight: Sunlight and moonlight have special uses. You can cure your impotence or frigidity and enhance your spiritual energy with the nutrition of the sun-shine. With moonlight, you can help your feminine energy or balance your masculine energy. [See pages 143–45; also con-sult *The Gentle Path of Spiritual Progress* by Hua-Ching Ni.]

Moonlight: Moonlight affects your intelligence. During the cycle from the new moon to the full moon, with each moonrise you should quietly sit or stand and watch it, and absorb the light to improve the condition of your intelligence. Only a few minutes, at its rising, are useful; other times can also help. In any case, do not use the light during the declining moon.

Starlight: Starlight is also helpful. If you feel you are attacked by evil spirits, you should quietly expose yourself to the light of the North Star and the Big Dipper. The starry energy will cleanse you and the evil spirits will quickly leave you because they cannot face the righteous power of these grouped stars. If you have been sick for a long time and find that general medicine does not help, then you should pray to the North Star during the time you are also under the care of good natural medical treatment. The North Star will help you. If you have done something you feel was wrong or improper, and it has troubled your soul, repent under the North Star and the Big Dipper. Do this as a secret practice. Or, if you are a person who respects your spiritual nature above everything else, and you have violated your spiritual nature, repent and pray to the North Star and the Big Dipper for the change you are going to make in yourself. If you have a personal wish which can seriously affect your spirituality or practical fortune, you can also pray to the North Star and the Big Dipper. If you live in the Southern Hemisphere, use the Southern Cross to help you. Although it is more gentle and not as strong or sharp, it is still very effective.

However, when you pray, be pure of heart, like a child, because with purity the natural energy easily responds to you. It is not like applying a complex intellectual formula; if you make yourself complicated, the corresponding natural energy cannot be reached. People want a better life, a good marriage, good children, good salary, health, longevity, and so forth; these are all at the level of being under the energies of the stars. Stars can usually help you if you are sincere in your intention. If your wish is simple, it is easy to achieve. The star energy can help you to cleanse your conscious condition through purifying your heart.

The intellectual star watcher can receive some benefit as well, but not much, because the purpose is so different. Watching the stars in this way is like studying geography. Remembering the names of the stars and having pride in your specific knowledge fails to make a connection with the spiritual energy; this is intellectual.

The star energy can take you flying. This may be hard for your intellectual mind to accept, but it is a beautiful discovery. In ancient times, a man was once wandering carelessly in the wilderness and fell into a big hole in the land. The walls of the hole were too steep for him to climb out. The man survived on some vegetation and herbs that were growing in the hole, so his body became light. Before very long, there was nothing left for him to do or try, because he had exhausted all attempts to get out. There were no longer any psychological burdens such as hope within him. No thoughts were left in his mind; because thoughts have weight and he was free of them, he became even lighter. Physically and mentally, he was very much changed by eating those particular herbs. The sun and moon did not pass over the hole, only the stars. He kept watching the stars because there was nothing else to watch. On a certain day, while watching them, the attraction of the energy of the stars lifted the man out of the hole. Afterwards, Taoists utilized the star energy and the strength of herbs to learn flying or at least to cause the ascension of internal spiritual energy.

Another way to levitate is by using a particular breathing system. The grandfather of Bao Po Tzu achieved it; he floated up to the ceiling and down many times. This is a different method than using the attraction of the stars to take you up.

Once you learn to use the natural energy of the stars,

please be respectful of it and yourself. Such a thing is powerful and serious when you are not yet experienced.

Darkness: Darkness also nourishes you. It can be used when asleep or resting in your room. It is especially helpful if you are weak, have lost a lot of blood, or have just given birth to a baby. All light from outside should be shut out, and the reflecting surfaces like mirrors and dressing tables covered. Any light will stimulate a person and not provide the peace that supports recovery. Just as the roots of most trees are in darkness; this darkness also supports your energy. Your nervous system needs rest. It needs an environment of no stimulation, no slight smell or light. [36:81–87]

Sun and Moon Practice

Now let us talk about how to utilize the energy of the sun and moon. We know that one of the best social welfare systems in the world today exists in Sweden, but Sweden also has a very high rate of suicide. Why is this? It is because their winters are too long and they do not get enough sun.

If you lived in a place without sunshine for six months, don't you think you would get depressed? If a mature woman was isolated and never saw a strong man, her life would have no light or warmth. It is important for people to have solar energy within and without. People commonly utilize the sunshine by going to the beach and baking themselves. Sometimes they overdo it and get freckles or even sunburn to the extent that they develop skin cancer. So this is not the way to do it. I want to show you how, in the great teaching of Tao, all people, but particularly women without men or men without women, can utilize the great energy of the sun and moon to balance themselves.

Men sometimes have lowered sexual energy and suffer impotence because of the tension caused by intellectual or emotional struggles in their life. Impotence is a kind of weakness. Every morning, when the sun rises, you should stand in a place with good air, face the east, and breathe in the solar energy. Swallow it and send it to the lower tan-t'ien, the place just below the navel. Even if it is cloudy, you can still do the practice. The sun is still there. By your spiritual development, you can make the sun energy come to you through the clouds.

Men who suffer from sexual weakness can use this practice to cure themselves. By doing this thirty times every morning, a man's strength can be restored within one to nine months. Nine swallows is the minimum practice. Thirty times qualifies you as a person of Tao who lives on more than just physical food alone.

How about women, now? Women are often not satisfied with their husbands, so they need a true husband who is always available. This is not a husband that will cause your first husband any jealousy, though, because it is the sun. At the most, a woman should breathe in the solar energy only nine times, otherwise she will become too manly. You need to balance yourself so that whether you have a man or not, you will not be unsatisfied or crave a man. You suffer without a man, but you suffer once you have one too. It is better to have the sun as your great husband and your other husband as refreshment. You will also increase your vitality in this way. This is the secret of men and women's practice. . . .

We have talked mostly about solar energy. Now, if you are interested, we will talk about the moon's energy.

The sun's energy is connected with masculine energy, and the moon's is connected with feminine energy. In general, the bodies of both men and women is mostly water, which is strongly affected by the moon's energy. In the fall, around the eighth lunar month, the ocean tides are strongest, because lunar energy attraction is stronger at that time. In ancient times, women's menstrual cycles began with the full moon, because when feminine energy is at its fullest it causes the blood vessels in the uterus to compensate for the increased pressure of the body's energy flow at that time by releasing some of the blood. If the regularity of this natural balance is blocked, emotional and physical stress and illness can occur. In today's society, with so many unnatural influences, most women's cycles no longer follow the phases of the moon. Some have no pattern of regularity at all.

The moon not only affects women's energy, it also affects all people's mental energy very much. The moon is your mind. People who are born near the time of the full moon are brighter, as a rule, than people born on the night of the new moon. If those born on the new moon do not have support from other energy sources, such as good spiritual inheritance, they will not be as smart. In general, intelligence is connected with the moon. You should not have sex, therefore, on a night with no moonlight, because if you conceive a child at that time, the baby's mind will not develop well. Actually, I do not recommend sex during either the full moon or no moon. As a special, beneficial practice, you could sit and do your quiet cultivation during the full moon, but not a meditation that involves deep thinking. In general, the full moon is very disturbing to the peace of the internal liquid of your body, but by cultivating nonmental activity at this time, you can do better.

Now I need to tell you how to use the moon's cycle to help your cultivation. You can take lunar energy in the same way as solar energy. You should begin at the time of the new moon and go until five days after the full moon. After that, the moon's energy is not strong any more.

If a woman knows how to utilize lunar energy, she will become very full of feminine energy and be very attractive. It is important to know how to guard and protect your good energy once you have gathered it, because other people and beings like to come around and take it. If you do not know how to guard yourself, then your energy can be destroyed and will need to be built up again. Ladies of Tao know how to make themselves young, even in old age, by increasing their energy without letting anyone take it away. Not only do men try to take this energy, but also spirits and human ghosts.

Ordinary houses have a spiritual house guardian, but you can be attacked by ghosts if you stay in motels or other public places, especially if you are a single person. If you have good energy, you need to take care of it.

To take in the moon's energy, you face the moon when it is just rising, gently breathe in the lunar energy and swallow it. If you do this faithfully for three years, your face will have a light. Natural energy can be accumulated and grow, so that when your body fails, you will have an energy house built from the natural energy you have gathered, along with your personal refined energy. You can then move into the subtle sphere of life as a heavenly being of light.

Men should swallow the lunar energy six times, and women should do it thirty times. If a woman is already too manly, she should utilize the lunar energy more. Even if a man is not very masculine, he can still do this practice along with the solar cultivation. [14:153–54, 166–68]

Friendly Advice

- Have trust in the constancy of the natural cyclic movement. In good times, do not be too excited, but foresee the downward slope; in bad times, do not be dismayed, because it will turn around. Nothing is stuck forever. (From Lao Tzu and Chuang Tzu)

- Attain the knowledge of the subtle law, which can be quietly observed: any trouble has its precondition. Thus, do not build the conditions for trouble, but quietly live with the subtle law. (From Lao Tzu and Chuang Tzu)

- Unite yourself with the impersonal Heaven; dissociate from the conceptual trap of undeveloped religion. Extend universal love and life without obstruction by personal, racial, or cultural background. (From Lao Tzu, Mo Tzu, and Chuang Tzu)

- Be kind and just to all. (From Lao Tzu, Confucius, Mo Tzu, and Chuang Tzu)

- Promote what is beneficial to the world, and do away with what is harmful to the world. This is the goal of a leader and teacher and person of influence. (From Mo Tzu)

- Do what is beneficial to the world, and do not do what is harmful to the world, on the basis of an individual. (From Chuang Tzu)

- Decrease the burden of the mind. Increase the unity of the body, mind, and spirit. (From Lao Tzu)

- Keep your body and mind moving and your spirit quiet. (From Lao Tzu)

- Strengthen your physical body; weaken your detrimental ambition. (From Lao Tzu)

- Be non-impulsive. (From Lao Tzu)

- Be practical and matter-of-fact; do not be fancy or crazy. (From Lao Tzu)

- Concentrate on the essential. (From Lao Tzu)

- Concentrate on the foundation. (From Lao Tzu and Confucius)

- Apply the golden mean to all levels of life, which means never go to the extreme in anything. (From Lao Tzu and Confucius)

- Be natural and accept what is natural; do not be artificial or accept what is artificially developed from the natural. (From Chuang Tzu)

- Be egoless. (From Chuang Tzu)

- Be objective. (From Chuang Tzu)

- Do not be argumentative, but look for harmony. (From Chuang Tzu)

- Do not be judgmental in speech; keep your discernment in the quiet of your mind. (From Chuang Tzu)

- Look at the balance point between spiritual selflessness and self-responsibility in all aspects of your life. (From the I Ching)

- Practice moderation in life, such as in food and sex. [2:466–67]

Sources and Resources

The books listed below, and other materials by Hua-Ching Ni (including audio and video tapes), are available from:

SevenStar Communications
1314 Second Street
Santa Monica, CA 90401

TEL.: (310) 576-1901
FAX: (310) 917-2267
E-MAIL: taostar@ix.netcom.com
HOME PAGE ADDRESS: http://www.taostar.com

For information about study groups, classes, mentorship, or teaching in the United States and around the world, contact:

Universal Society of the Integral Way (USIW)
P.O. Box 28993
Atlanta, GA 30358-0993

The USIW also produces a quarterly newsletter with activities and news related to the teachings of the Integral Way.

For a correspondence course, contact the SevenStar home page address above or write to:

The Integral Way of Life Correspondence Course
P.O. Box 1222
El Prado, NM 87529

Anyone interested in in-depth learning of traditional Chinese medicine may contact:

Yo San University of Traditional Chinese Medicine
1314 Second Street
Santa Monica, CA 90401

TEL.: (310) 917-2202
FAX: (310) 917-2203

The university accepts students from around the world and also has a financial aid program.

1. *Ageless Counsel for Modern Times* (1992). Commentaries on the *I Ching*.

2. *Attaining Unlimited Life* (1989). The wisdom of Chuang Tzu.

3. *Attune Your Body with Dao-in* (1992; revised ed. 1994).

4. *The Book of Changes and the Unchanging Truth (I Ching)* (1983; 2nd ed. 1990)

5. *The Complete Works of Lao Tzu* (1979). Includes the *Tao Teh Ching* and the *Hua Hu Ching*. (The *Hua Hu Ching* is also available in an edition from Shambhala Publications.)

6. *Concourse of All Spiritual Paths* (1995)

7. *Eight Thousand Years of Wisdom*, vol. 1 (1983)

8. *Eight Thousand Years of Wisdom*, vol. 2 (1983)

9. *Enlightenment: Mother of Spiritual Independence* (1989). The story of Hui-neng.

10. *Esoteric Tao Teh Ching* (1993)

11. *Essence of Universal Spirituality* (1990)

12. *Eternal Light* (1991)

13. *Footsteps of the Mystical Child* (1986)

14. *The Gentle Path of Spiritual Progress* (1990).

15. *Golden Message* (1993). Outlines a program of study of the Integral Way.

16. *Guide to Inner Light* (1990)

17. *Guide to Your Total Well-Being* (1994). Booklet.

18. *Harmony: The Art of Life* (1992)

19. *Heavenly Way: The Union of Tao and Universe* (1981). Booklet.

20. *Internal Alchemy* (1992)

21. *Internal Growth through Tao* (1991)

22. *The Key to Good Fortune* (1991)

23. *Less Stress, More Happiness* (1994). Booklet.

24. *Life and Teachings of Two Immortals*, vol. 1: *Kou Hong* (1992)

25. *Life and Teachings of Two Immortals*, vol. 2: *Chen Tuan* (1993)

26. *The Light of All Stars Illuminates the Way* (1994). Booklet.

27. *Moonlight in the Dark Night* (1992)

28. *The Mystical Universal Mother* (1992)

29. *Mysticism* (1992)

30. *Nurture Your Spirits* (1991)

31. *The Power of Natural Healing* (1991)

32. *Progress along the Way: Life, Service, and Realization* (1994). Booklet.

33. *Quest of Soul* (1991)

34. *Spiritual Messages from a Buffalo Rider* (1990)

35. *Stepping Stones for Spiritual Progress* (1990)

36. *The Story of Two Kingdoms* (1989)

37. *Strength from Movement: Mastering Chi* (1994)

38. *Tao, the Subtle Universal Law* (1979)

39. *The Taoist Inner View of the Universe* (1979)

40. *The Time Is Now for a Better Life and a Better World* (1992)

41. *The Uncharted Voyage toward the Subtle Light* (1985)

42. *The Way of Integral Life* (1989)

43. *The Way, the Truth, and the Light* (1993)

44. *Workbook for Spiritual Development* (1984; revised ed. 1995)

Index